ALIA'S VOICE

A Syrian Refugee in Canada

Published in Canada.

Cover designed by: John of Flocksy Inc.

Photo credits:
Figures 1, 2, 3, 7, 14, N.Hori, Mississauga, Ontario.
Figure 4, K. Hori, Mississauga, Ontario.
Figures 6, 7, 9, 10, 11,17, Ann McRae, Dundas, Ontario.
Figure 16, Jim Cairney, Dundas, Ontario.
Figures 8, 12, 15, 16, J. Webber, Winnipeg, Manitoba.
Figure 13, A. Al Rmidain
Author's portrait, back cover, Jim Cairney, Dundas, Ontario.

ISBN: 978-1-990728-05-1 Alia's Voice A Syrian Refugee in Canada Digital-PDF
ISBN: 978-1-990728-04-4 Alia's Voice A Syrian Refugee in Canada Paperback
ISBN: 978-1-990728-03-7 Alia's Voice A Syrian Refugee in Canada Hardcover book
ISBN: 978-1-990728-02-0 Alia's Voice A Syrian Refugee in Canada Audio Book
ISBN: 978-1-990728-01-3 Alia's Voice A Syrian Refugee in Canada E-Book

Library and Archives Canada Cataloguing in Publication
Title: Alia's Voice: A Syrian Refugee in Canada / by E. Ann McRae
Names: McRae, Elizabeth Ann, 1953 -
Identifiers: Biography, Syrian refugees.

The characters and events in this book are factual. Names of some individuals have been changed for reasons of privacy.

DEDICATION

This book is dedicated to the teams of volunteers across Canada who helped to welcome refugees into their communities. It is also dedicated to the government workers, both overseas and in Canada, to church organizations, English teachers and social workers, all of whom made this story possible.

PREFACE

The characters and locations in this book are real. For privacy reasons, some names have been changed. Beyond that, a large measure of artistic license was applied to compress a lifetime into just a small book.

For background information on the Syrian civil war and on Canadian immigration procedures, the research is my own, and I bear the responsibility for any inaccuracies.

The rest of the information in this book was gathered in the usual way, allowing for COVID restrictions: I began by interviewing Alia at length, during her summer vacation at the cottage that is featured in some chapters. The words are mine, but the tone, ideas, memories and descriptions are hers.

I interviewed several of the support committee volunteers at the picnic mentioned in the citizenship chapter, as well as by phone, or by email, or by a combination of these. I assigned portions of the story to "narrator" voices, including Alia's.

In the Canadian section of the story, a half-dozen voices of Canadian friends, real people identified by first names only, stand in for more than a dozen volunteers of all ages who assisted the Al Rmidains on many levels. The comments attributed to the Canadians, like those attributed to Alia, are compilations, not quotes. All incidents described actually happened.

EAM

TABLE OF CONTENTS

TURKEY

⊙Aleppo

● Abu Adh Dhuhur

SYRIA

CYPRUS

Zahlé

Beirut⊙
LEBANON

⊙Damascus

IRAQ

MEDITERRANEAN
SEA

ISRAEL

Tel Aviv⊙

JORDAN

0   100 200 250

SCALE IN KMS.

BEGINNINGS

BACKGROUND

On Thursday, August 4, 2016, Alia and Hussein and their four children arrived at Toronto Pearson airport and began a new life in Canada. Their journey through the new language and culture made both of them into different people in the space of just three years. Hussein's journey by road and air was the same distance as Alia's, in kilometres, but by other measures, Alia came much farther. Her journey is the focus of this book.

The drama begins in Syria, of course. The second half unfolds in Canada, against the backdrop of the Canadian government's refugee sponsorship structure. This plan encouraged citizen groups to partner with the government in bringing refugee families to Canada and helping them get established.

There is a chapter giving a thumbnail sketch of the war in Syria. For this story to make sense, a little background about that conflict is necessary. Avid readers of international news and politics may wish to skip that chapter. Others may want a refresher.

A group of volunteers in Mississauga, Ontario, played a huge role in this story. They got together and formed a refugee sponsorship committee. Readers familiar with the refugee process will not need to read the chapter that gives a quick tour of refugee sponsorship and its jargon.

In the first half of the story, I have not quoted Alia, but have reframed my interview notes as if she were telling a continuous story. She has graciously allowed me this liberty.

In the Canadian section of the book, I have attributed entire chapters to members of the team of volunteers. Although some narration is in the first person, I have tried to avoid quoting anyone. Instead, I have incorporated their experiences and reflections into the narrative. No part of this text should be read as a direct quote from anyone other than the author.

THE SOUNDS OF WAR

This is a joyful story, but it arises from adversity. The bitter taste of leaving one's home, possibly never to return, lingers.

Stories of refugees from different wars fill the front pages of newspapers, as this book was being completed. Faced with new terrors, the world begins to forget the evils of the Syrian civil war, and yet its effects will be felt for decades on the families such as Alia's and Hussein's. Millions are still displaced within and outside of Syria. The word "millions" is mind-numbing, and inadequate to express the human suffering, the struggle of families and individuals. In many cases, these people have no prospect of return. To call them "refugees" is not to comment on their legal status, but only to note that they are seeking a place of safety, a refuge, inside or outside of Syria.

The background sounds of war remain in one's memory, once refugees get to a safe place. Despair and worry for the loved ones left behind occupy a dark place in the mind. While we celebrate with those who successfully begin a new life, we cannot assume that they have really left everything behind. Some are able to put the past behind them most of the time. Many can never fully escape those memories, the mental and emotional wounds of war.

THE WAR IN SYRIA

For people to seek refuge, there is usually some monstrous force that drives them away from the homes they love. The monster in Alia's story is the sprawling, unending Syrian civil war.

Complex geographic, historic and political factors caused the war, far more complex than what can be captured in a few pages. The chaos and damage inflicted on the Syrian people, their cities, homes and livelihoods will not heal for a long time, if ever. The conflict generated the world's largest humanitarian crisis in decades.

Aleppo, the city of Alia's childhood, was a rebel stronghold, and as such, was bombed into ruins by the Syrian air force over a lengthy campaign. Her immediate family no longer lived there when war broke out, but some members of her extended family continued to stay there, even under bombardment. Government forces recaptured the city in 2016, by which time it was largely in ruins.

The people living in the middle of a war do not always receive reliable explanations about why it is happening. They know only of the impact: They know of deaths, of family members lost, of neighbourhoods, homes and even farms destroyed. They live with shortages and embargoes, with schools closed, empty shelves in stores, and increasing numbers of men being conscripted to feed the machinery of war. By the thousands, Syrians sought safety for their families in the countryside. When that proved to be equally unsafe, they crossed into neighbouring countries.

A refugee "problem" takes time to become a crisis, time before it warrants international attention. In Syria, problems began in 2011, and then gained momentum.

In that year, several Arab-majority countries, notably Egypt, experienced popular uprisings collectively known as the Arab Spring. Activists appealed to their own governments for changes, for more freedoms, for more accountability, and for human rights.

The intoxicating breeze of Arab Spring wafted through Syria, where it was inhaled by those dissatisfied with the regime of President Bashir al-Assad. Riding a wave of optimism, they hoped to get enough popular and even international support to nudge the Syrian government toward democratization. However, in Syria, as in other nations, the backlash against popular movements led the nervous government to tighten, not to loosen, its grip on areas of unrest.

President al-Assad responded to the perceived threat by bombing and gassing Syrian civilians in areas suspected of protecting his opponents. This caused some noisy scolding in the international press, but no other significant consequences. Even messy, un-civil civil wars are considered the internal business of a nation, so on-lookers did little, at first.

Divisions arose along religious lines (Sunni-Shia) as well as ethnic lines, such as the Kurdish independence movement. Before the war, many Syrian families, like Alia's, were unaware of, or indifferent to, which neighbours were Sunnis and which were Shia Muslims. Little distinction was made, until ISIS fighters from other countries began bringing sectarian divisions to the fore. Various external players saw their moment to put their own interests forward: Russia, Turkey, Iran, and the Islamic State known variously as ISIL, ISIS, or Daesh. Neighbouring countries, worried about the stability of the region, provided support to one side or the other. This effectively enlarged the conflict, rather than helping to resolve it.

The citizens in large areas of Syria were supportive of the President, but this did not save them from being caught in a cross-fire. The Syrian army and the opposition groups fought for control of key cities and towns. Fighting displaced some six million Syrians within the country's borders, while another five and a half million sought refuge in other countries[1].

Other books have been written, and will be written, about this conflict, which is still unfolding.

---

[1] Figures are from the Government of Canada's **Syrian Outcomes Report, May 2019.**

A PHOTO WORTH A THOUSAND WORDS

On September 2, 2015, a Turkish photojournalist captured an image that went around the world. He photographed the drowned body of Alan Kurdi, a two-year-old Syrian boy, lying face-down on a pebble beach. He died when the small boat carrying his parents, brother and many other refugees, capsized. His mother and brother also died.

Young Alan Kurdi and his family were among thousands of families seeking a route to Europe. They attempted to cross a stretch of the Mediterranean between Turkey and Greece.

The press reported that the Kurdi family had pinned their hopes on getting to Canada, where they had relatives. That detail made the tragedy all the more riveting for Canadian readers.

The image of a dead child, along with other photos capturing the anguish of Alan's father, vaulted the Syrian refugee situation onto the front pages of newspapers in Canada and around the world. A howl of pain and outrage went up from ordinary Canadians. In response, the government of Canada created a program of sponsorship in the fall of 2015.

THE WHEELS BEGIN TO TURN

Public pressure on Canadian parliamentarians resulted in a commitment by the government to bring twenty-five thousand Syrians to Canada. Some were to be sponsored by the government, some by private citizen groups, and others in a blended program of government and private sector assistance. The Al Rmidain family was selected for the last category.

In the fall of 2015, the Canadian government undertook to bring refugees to Canada as soon as November of 2015. The backlog of applicants in Canadian overseas offices was enormous.

Canadians were offered the opportunity to form community groups to sponsor a family. Canada's larger church organizations (Catholic, United, Presbyterian, Anglican and others) created offices and programs to guide and support the sponsorship groups. Many other large and small organizations, including many mosques, Jewish synagogues and other faith groups, as well as many with no religious affiliation, pitched in to encourage the formation of sponsorship groups and to support their fundraising efforts.

Hundreds of groups formed almost overnight. A deluge of paperwork landed at Canada's embassies and consulates overseas, primarily in Lebanon. Consular workers were charged with matching up community groups and families in need.

Sponsoring groups were required to demonstrate their ability to carry out their obligations by raising enough funds in advance to support a family for a year. In addition, the community groups needed to have enough volunteers with time available to help the families get established, get to medical and other appointments, get to English classes and so on.

Not since the Vietnamese refugee crisis in the 1970s had so many Canadian churches, community groups and individuals been involved in such a commitment. The government of Canada has posted its summary of the Syrian refugee programs and their outcomes at a link which is operational at the time of writing, but may need updating: Syrian Outcomes Report May 2019.

SPONSORSHIP: NAVIGATING THE JARGON

Volunteers new to refugee work struggle with the language of bureaucracy. They learn, for example, that "**sponsorship**" refers to the financial and other tangible assistance provided to refugees. Assistance is necessary because the Geneva Convention, described in more detail below, gives the framework to Canada's refugee policy. An international treaty, the Convention leads us to accept refugees into Canada without a demonstration of their financial self-sufficiency. This is in sharp contrast to other types of immigrants to Canada.

In general, people applying to be Canadian residents must demonstrate language ability, education and job skills, or the financial resources to create a job for themselves and employ others. However, the Geneva Convention of 1946 recognizes that those fleeing persecution and war are not like other immigrants. They need to be able to find a place of safety first, and then work their way toward these other self-sufficiency goals.

"**Settlement**" refers to the process of acclimatizing new arrivals to their new homeland. This includes language training, assistance with finding housing, and connecting the new arrivals with health care, dental care, schools, counselling and other services. Every large city in Canada has non-profit agencies committed to delivering settlement services. In smaller centres, there is more of a patchwork of services, offered by smaller local organizations.

"**Refugee**," in the chapters that follow, refers to a person not simply look-ing for a place of safety, but identified by the United Nations as a person "in need of protection," under the Geneva Convention. The Convention, dating back to the post-World War II period and the League of Nations, reflects the concerns of Canada's allies in 1946, and contains the funda-mental definition of "refugee" used in many countries including Canada. While some modifications have been made in the decades since 1946, the definition is essentially unchanged.

Those whose cases are screened and approved overseas, either by United Nations officers, or by staff at Canadian embassies and consulates over-seas, arrive in Canada as legal residents, and do not go through any further evaluation of their refugee case.

There is an important difference between those who arrive in Canada as UN refugees and those who have no such approval: the latter must claim refugee status upon or after arrival, and will be required to prove their case. UN-approved refugees arrive in Canada holding permanent-resident visas. Their qualification for refugee status has already been approved.

Despite this government stamp of approval, UN-approved refugees are sometimes viewed with the same suspicion that is directed at those who enter by land from the United States, and have not yet proved their cases. This unwarranted suspicion can make new arrivals hesitant to let their refugee status be known.

Much has been written on the finer points of refugee law and process. In this account, it is assumed that all Syrian refugees in Canada, those arriving through airports, have already had their cases determined by the United Nations High Commission for Refugees (UNHCR) or by Canadian dip-lomatic staff in the field, before they were referred to a Canadian consular office for processing and travel to Canada.

Unlike asylum-seekers who present themselves at Canada's borders, the Syrian refugees in this story did not face the uncertainty of persuading Canadian authorities, upon arrival, of their claim to permanent residence. That step was accomplished before they boarded a flight to Canada.

PART ONE

MY LIFE IN SYRIA

I am Alia.

I want my Canadian friends and my own children to know how family life in Syria was, before the war changed everything for us. It was a good life, in many ways. Although I miss so many things, I cannot go back. I will not go back. It is not because of what we lost in the war, although that breaks my heart. It is because my life has changed. I have changed.

It would be impossible for me to be that person that I was. I will try to explain it, but first, I must tell about my old life, a typical Syrian life, a happy life.

My father and mother, Hamdo and Dooha, had twelve children. I was the tenth. One sister, Iman, and one brother, Hussein, are younger than I am. Hussein would be called a "special needs" person in Canada. He cannot take care of himself, and lives with my widowed mother.

My other brothers are Ahmed, Mahmoud, Jamma, Mohamed and Kaled. My older sisters are Aisha, Aziza, Fatima. Large families, and therefore large homes, are fairly common in Syria.

During my early childhood, my father worked at construction, building houses, in the city of Aleppo.

Our house, and most houses in Aleppo, indeed in most of Syria, are built of concrete blocks or poured concrete, using steel bars for reinforcement. A family starts with one or more rooms, and adds more rooms depending on the needs of the family. The rooms form a square around a central garden space.

Sons who marry generally live in the family house. The family adds a room for the young couple, and after there are children, another room may be added for the children. Daughters-in-law customarily join their husband's family, living with their in-laws in a large family cluster. My sisters lived at my parents' home until they married, then they moved out. Two of the older ones had moved out before I really got to know them.

Syrian houses have flat roofs, usually with a large water tank on the roof, which is filled from a water truck as needed.

There is a common kitchen, and the cooking is shared, but it often falls to the younger daughters and the daughters-in-law to do the cooking and housekeeping for the older couple and all the men, as well as the children, of course. In my childhood experience, it was unusual for women to have work outside of the home, although one may have some side income from sewing, as I did when we moved to Lebanon. But I am going to tell you the story about Syria, first.

Our city home was perfect, to me. We had a large, central room, where we could all eat. If the weather was good, we could sit in the inner courtyard or garden for meals, as well as for entertaining.

Syrian families do not gather around a table, as we learned to do in Canada. Instead, we have low furniture and pillows around the outside of the room, for sitting. Food is prepared and brought in large bowls, which are placed on a cloth that is spread in the middle of the floor. The floor would usually be carpeted, unless we were entertaining in the open courtyard in the centre of the house.

The younger women would wait on the men, and perhaps on the older women. Children would be fed separately.

Everything that we needed could be obtained within a short distance of our house, so owning a car was not necessary. We could buy bread, vegetables, meat and anything else from small shops in our neighbourhood. My brothers worked with my father in construction.

I went to a school where both boys and girls studied, near our house in Aleppo. I was a good student. I enjoyed school and was proud of doing well.

OUR FARM

One day, when I was about twelve, my parents told me we were leaving Aleppo, and moving back to the rural area where my father's family had lived for a long time. My father had been doing heavy construction work for many years, since he was a young man. He was ready for a change. When we moved to the country, we would be farmers.

I was disappointed to discover that I would not be able to go to school after we moved. There was a school for rural children, but I couldn't go to it because it would involve a bus ride. By custom in rural Syria, children and young women do not travel alone on buses. A male family member such as an older brother or father or uncle would have to go with me. So, although there were nice things about living in the country, it put an end to my education.

The teacher at my old school in Aleppo tried to persuade my mother to let me stay in school, somehow. She wrote a letter to my mother, telling her that I was a very good student, and that I could "become something." She didn't offer any suggestions about what sort of "something." I suppose she knew that I would become a wife and mother, and then not be able to get any further education, which is what happened. It was many years before I had a chance to return to school, but that comes later in this story.

My father sold our big house in Aleppo. The house and land were valuable because they were in the centre of the city, close to everything. The new owner built an apartment building, and gave two of the new units to my father, as part of the purchase arrangement. One apartment was occupied by my married brother and his wife. The other apartment we rented out.

From the age of twelve, with no school, my main job was to help my mother at home. Of my sisters, only Iman was still at home, and she helped my mother, too. I had five brothers at home, one of whom, Mahmoud, was married. His wife also helped. My oldest brother, Ahmed, was also married, but he lived in Aleppo in one of our apartments. So, with my father, there were five working men in our household. When they came home, food was served by the women: my mother, me, my sister Iman and my sister-in-law.

When we first moved to that house, it had only two rooms, plus a big hall for meals. This hall was paved, and roofed, but open on one side. We built six more rooms, to accommodate all the family members.

We had a cistern for water. City people did not have this. It meant that our water was cooler than it would be in a tank on the sunny rooftop.

Some of my father's relatives lived quite close by: my aunt Aisha lived in a house a few hundred metres away, not a long walk. Her husband worked in construction in Lebanon.

In those days, travel between Syria and other neighbouring countries was easy. People like my uncle went where they could find work. He would travel back and forth from his home to his work. It would take a day of bus travel, so he would not get home every week.

When my father worked in construction, he would have the supplies for each job delivered to the site by a truck. Then he would take a portable concrete mixer to the job site, and make concrete as the job went along.

He also worked in a mine where lime was extracted, using dynamite and pick axes. Both mining and construction were very heavy work, so it was easier for him when we moved to the farm.

On our farm, which was about a fifteen-minute drive from Aleppo, there were olive trees in abundance. They had been planted at least thirty years earlier, perhaps much earlier. It takes olive trees a long time to grow to a productive size, but then they keep on producing for many years. Olive trees are some of the oldest trees in our area.

Just before winter, which in Syria means a cooler season with rain, the olives would be ready to harvest. Everybody -- men, women and children -- would go out to pick the olives, from eight o'clock in the morning until three. We would load a truck with olives, and then the men would drive it to the olive press. It was not far, but we had to get an appointment, because everyone had olives ready for pressing at the same time.

When our time came, our crop would be pressed into olive oil. In a good year, we could get fifty barrels, each with twenty kilograms of olive oil. In addition, we would set aside some olives to preserve in jars, and eat with each meal.

For me and my family, olive oil is part of almost every meal. It is an ingredient in salads, in humus, in tahini sauce, and many other dishes. Later in my life, in Canada, I was surprised to discover that every kitchen did not have a large supply of olive oil. Even more surprising was the discovery that some Canadians have never eaten an olive with a stone. They are familiar only with the ones preserved with a slice of red pepper in the middle. Later I will talk about the little surprises and the big surprises about life in Canada.

When our olive oil was harvested and put into twenty-kilogram barrels, we borrowed a wagon from my aunt Aisha, the one who lived nearby, and transported the oil to our house. We used it to trade or to sell to people we knew, as well as for gifts, and to supply our own kitchen.

Olives were not our only crop. There were grain crops, of the sort that do not require a lot of moisture, because we did not irrigate. Wheat can grow all year round, in Syria. We also grew barley, red lentils, black lentils, chickpeas and red beans. My aunt Aisha had almond trees, too.

In the city house, our central garden was restricted to growing flowers, because we could readily obtain all the vegetables we needed at shops. At the farm, there was a garden for herbs, and every imaginable vegetable: zucchini, eggplant, watermelon, cucumber, onions, and lots of tomatoes. We irrigated these vegetables, otherwise there would not be enough natural rainfall in the area for them to thrive.

We ate tomatoes and cucumber at almost every meal. We also preserved tomatoes in jars, first making them into a thick paste. This would be used in sauces with pasta or in stews.

Although we have a cooler season called "winter," it is not like winter in colder climates. On a sunny day in Syrian winter, it would be comfortable to be outside, but it would not be hot.

I do not remember any vacations or travel, other than to visit relatives who lived in Lebanon. Everyone has Friday off, because it is the Muslim holy day.

Most men in my family did not go to mosque for Friday prayers, although some families did. Women do not go to mosque, but do their prayers at home.

My family often entertained, and I still love to do this in Canada. In Syria, my family would invite another family to share a meal with us almost every week. The biggest gatherings of relatives happened at the festival of Eid, at the end of the holy month of Ramadan. Hussein and I tried to continue this sort of hospitality when we got married.

I was born in 1986. I was eighteen when I got married, in 2004. The war started about six years later.

I did not know much about the war. It began in a city called Dara. My father had died just before the war started, so there were a lot of changes for our household, and no one talked to me about the war.

MY FATHER'S DEATH

My father's health had deteriorated for a year before he died, but he would not seek medical help. He was between fifty-five and sixty. It was shocking how the illness started with him: He was thirsty, and I gave him a glass of water, but he swallowed it the wrong way and began to choke. Then, almost instantly, his voice was gone, and he could not make a sound for four days. He had no pain, but after losing his voice for four days, my mother persuaded him to go to Aleppo to see a doctor.

We expected him to stay overnight with my brother Ahmed, who lived in the apartment in Aleppo, and return to the farm the next day. That is not what happened.

Ahmed advised us that our father couldn't come back, as he was too sick. The doctors told him he had lung cancer. It must have been very advanced, to take away his voice like that. My mother decided to travel to Aleppo to see him. She went by herself. An older woman is safer to travel by bus, so that was acceptable, but unusual.

By the time she got there, he was in a hospital bed. She wanted to get someone to drive him home, so that she could take care of him, but he was determined that the family would not see him in a weakened state, and refused to cooperate. He still had no voice, and was coughing blood by the time she saw him.

After many appointments with many doctors, and all sorts of tests, they determined that he was beyond treatment. There was nothing that could be done, except pain medication.

Ahmed knew it was cancer, but didn't tell anyone. My father kept insisting he would get better. Finally, my mother took him home and he stayed at home for three months. There was a period when he seemed to be getting slightly better. He was still short of breath, and could not talk, but was a bit stronger. Then he began to lose the ability to walk.

We took him to a physiotherapist to get help with his walking, but it turned out that the cancer was affecting his nerves. Soon he needed help walking, and could not get to the bathroom by himself. He refused help. He asked to be taken to hospital, rather than have his family take care of him. He refused to see visitors, while he was there, not even my sister and me. He kept insisting he was fine, and would be back.

After ten days in hospital, he died. At first my mother had wanted to stay at the hospital with him, but she could not, because she was needed at home to care for my handicapped brother, Hussein. Toward the end, she decided to entrust Hussein's care to Iman and me, so that she could be with my father for his last days.

My father's stubbornness added to the grief of losing him, and my heart still hurts. I was only eighteen. In his dignity and pride, he is typical of men in my culture.

His death happened just after I had met my future husband, also named Hussein, like my brother. I was planning to marry Hussein, but our engagement did not follow the usual pattern of preparations and pre-marriage celebrations, due to my father's illness and death.

My mother stayed at the farm after my father died, until the war started, about six years later. It was no longer safe at the farm. My mother fled to Efreen, a city that is near Turkey. She lives there still, with my brother Hussein. Some of my cousins and other relatives stayed in Aleppo, where life became harder and harder as the war went on.

GETTING MARRIED

All men over eighteen in Syria have to serve in the army for two and a half years. This was true before the war broke out. Later, as the war increased, all eligible men were required to serve again, even if they had already served their required period of two and a half years.

Before the war began, one of my brothers was doing his army service far from our farm, during the time that my father was sick. My brother needed my father to send him money, and needed to get this message to my father. He could not come home and speak to my father because he did not have leave. Instead, my brother sent another soldier, his friend Hussein Al Rmidain, because Hussein had the necessary three days of leave and was willing to travel to our farm. Hussein's family is related to mine, and he has the same last name as my father. He knew of my father, but had never met the rest of our family.

Hussein showed up at our house and delivered the message to my father. He saw me, and then decided he would make more visits to our house, when he had days off from his army service.

Hussein's home, in a city called Abu Adh Duhur, was near to where one of my married sisters, Amina, was living with her husband. Hussein arranged to bring Amina to visit my parents. My parents had previously met Hussein, because they had visited both Amina and my other married sister, Aziz, who also lived near Abu Adh Duhur

After several visits of this type, Hussein expressed to my father his interest in marrying me. He was good looking, and had some skills as a welder. My father was impressed, and agreed.

For my mother, this was a time of upheaval. In the year that I was married, my two remaining single brothers were also married, on the same day, two weeks after me. This meant that two new daughters-in-law moved into my mother's home. Then, my sister, Iman, the last one at home, was married. Both Iman and I would live with our husbands' families, no longer at home, so more of the burden of care of my handicapped brother fell on my mother, but also on my new sisters-in-law.

After I was married and moved away, my mother stayed with my younger brother Hussein at our farm near Aleppo, but it soon became too dangerous. Eventually my mother took my disabled brother and moved to the city I mentioned, Efreen, also known as Nisibis. Her sister lives there. My mother is still living there with my brother. She survives on whatever small amounts of money her children can send to her. Many people who needed to relocate were not so fortunate, and had no family members who could take them in.

Hussein's work was not at all nearby, so after we were married, we did not live near Aleppo. He worked at a welding shop in Abu Adh Duhur. His parents had lived there at one time, but they had migrated to Lebanon just a few years earlier. Hussien's father found better work in Lebanon than he had in Abu Adh Duhur.

HUSSEIN'S WORK IN ABU ADH DUHUR

In Abu Adh Duhur, in Syria, Hussein worked at a shop that welded almost anything. The shop made beds, frames and grills for doors and windows, and water tanks. The roof-top tanks that most homes relied upon for drinking water were made of metal in those days, as were the supports that held them in place. Some more modern buildings have plastic or fiberglass tanks.

While Hussein was working at the welding shop, both before and during the time that he was in the army, customers would bring in cars, trucks and trailers for welding work. The managers saw that Hussein was good at fixing cars and trucks, so they asked him to do vehicle repairs as well as general welding. Hussen had learned auto mechanics when he was in school, and these skills were in high demand.

During his army service, he worked at the shop on his days off, except when he was courting me. His employer, who was a Christian, liked him and liked his work. It was common for Christian businessmen to hire Muslims, just as it was common for Muslim business owners to hire Christians. In Syria and also in Lebanon, I did not notice any great hostility among religions.

Hussein and I moved to Lebanon when the war started. We already had our first child, a daughter, Amal. It did not take Hussein long to find welding work, but he wanted to be in Abu Adh Duhur, where he had a better job, so we came back after a short time. Also, there was a conflict between Israel and Lebanon, and it actually seemed safer in Syria.

The war in Syria seemed far away from Abu Adh Duhur, and did not affect us much, at the beginning. Travel between Syria and Lebanon was not a problem, at that time. Later it became difficult to go back and forth.

Our life in Abu Adh Duhur was tolerable, but owing to the war, the schools were closed. By this time, we had a daughter and a son, Amal and Ahmed, just over a year apart.

When they were both of school age, Hussein's mother came from Lebanon for a visit. She saw that the schools were closed because of the war, and insisted that Amal and Ahmed should live with her in Lebanon, so that they could attend school. Hussein didn't want to leave his job, where he was busy, and his boss really appreciated his skills. He wasn't sure what he would find in Lebanon.

My mother-in-law persuaded me to come to Lebanon on a "visit" with Amal and Ahmed, and the new baby, Amani. The older children could stay with her, she explained, when I returned home with little Amani. This was simpler than any formal arrangements that we could have made.

As a result, Amal and Ahmed began their schooling in the Lebanese fashion: they learned in Arabic and in French. Lebanon was formerly under French control, and is still part of the group of French-speaking nations. At the time, we had no idea that the French language could later be a useful part of their education.

I returned to Abu Adh Duhur with our youngest child, Amani, who was about two years old, and lived with Hussein there. It was about three years before all of us moved to Lebanon. We seldom saw the older children during this period, which I found very difficult.

There was some adjusting when the family could be reunited, because the older children's memory of Hussein and me had faded over that three-year period. Amani, who was a toddler when I returned to Abu Adh Duhur, had no memory of her older brother and sister.

One of the nerve-wracking features of living in Abu Adh Duhur was the sound of distant bombing. Once the war was close enough to hear bombardment, one could never escape the vague fear that it would gradually come closer, and that we might have to move.

There was an airport only a short distance from us which was used by the military, so war planes were coming and going on a regular basis. Still, daily life went on, with lots of work for Hussein and his boss, and lots of people still living in Abu Adh Duhur.

We did not really know what was happening, of course. There were probably radio and newspaper reports, but we did not know who to believe. I did not read or listen to the news. People talked among themselves, but it wasn't wise to express a strong opinion about one side or the other. It was safer to stay neutral and go about your business, as well as you could.

Fighters on both sides were getting killed. Families were losing sons and brothers. More and more men were being called to active service. And of course, we knew there were civilian casualties because people would talk about missing relatives.

We could not see any actual fighting from our home in Abu Adh Duhur. Sometimes, in the distance, we could see lines of vehicles moving men and equipment to different locations. We could not be sure if they were retreating or advancing, or who they were. Then the rebels, who had heavy guns but no aircraft, started shelling the airport near our home. Obviously, they wished to limit the Syrian army from using the airfield to launch bombing raids against rebel-held positions. Our daughter Amani grew up with the sound of shelling, a constant booming in the distance.

During this time, Hussein's mother came for a visit, from Lebanon, bringing Amal to see me and Hussein. My mother-in-law was horrified to discover that the sound of war was a constant presence. She argued with Hussein about living in a dangerous place. He had become used to it, and did not want to go to Lebanon, as it would mean looking for a new job.

His mother insisted that Amani and I should return with her. I agreed with her, fearing that our luck would turn one day soon. I thought we needed to be in a safer place, where we could be together with our children. I also missed seeing Amal and Ahmed grow up. I packed and travelled to Lebanon with my mother-in-law, taking Amani.

At the time, I did not know that I was pregnant with our fourth child. Our son, Musa, was born after I had lived in Lebanon for eight months.

Hussein stayed in Abu Adh Duhur after I left, until his boss decided it was not safe any longer. The boss closed the shop, packed up his family and travelled to Lebanon. Hussein came to Lebanon, to Zahlé, at the same time. That was four or five months after I left, so Hussein arrived in Lebanon at his parents' apartment in time to settle in before Musa's birth.

It was strange for me to join in this household. My older children viewed me as a sort of stranger, and called me by my usual nickname, "Sana," which is what the adults called me. In Syria and Lebanon I was generally known by this nickname. Nobody called me "Alia" until I came to Canada, another change!

I found it troubling that my older children called Hussein's mother "Mama," although she was their grandmother. This did not change when I joined the household, which was very difficult for me.

Amani did not know Amal and Ahmed at all, which was also an adjustment: she was used to being an only child! Amani continued to have nightmares about bombings, after we settled in Lebanon.

As Musa, the baby, learned to talk by imitating his older siblings, he also called me "Sana," when I would have preferred "Mama."

While Hussein stayed back in Abu Adh Duhur at his job, he was able to travel to see us a few times. It took one whole day to make the journey, in a van that carried fifteen people. This was a form of public transit. During this period, travelling back and forth across the border with Lebanon was not a problem.

Later, after Hussein had also moved to Zahlé, it became impossible for him to cross the border into Syria. As a visitor, he did not have papers to stay in Lebanon permanently. All available men of his age were being called up for active military duty in the Syrian army, even though he had already served his mandatory two and a half years.

Nobody wanted to be forced to go to the battle front because it was a war of brothers and cousins shooting brothers and cousins. Still, if he tried to resist serving in the army, the authorities would assume he was a rebel and a terrorist, and it would not go well for him. So, once he had found work in Zahlé, he only hoped to be able to support our family until it was safe for him to return. His plan was to return to live and work in Syria, once the risk of being sent to his death in battle was over.

For me, the hardest thing about adapting to Lebanon, aside from more than four months of being far from Hussein for the first time in our married life, was that I became the servant of everyone in the household of Hussein's parents. This had not been my role since I had lived in my own parent's home, before marriage.

Now I was the cook and housekeeper for Hussein's parents and younger brother, as well as Hussein's parents and of course my own children. Added to my new duties, I was pregnant when I arrived in Zahlé, and soon had a newborn to look after. I was frequently exhausted.

Being displaced by the war was difficult in ways that I had not foreseen, but it was not as miserable for me as it was for those with no relatives established in Lebanon.

Hussein's parents had lived in Zahlé for several years, and my father-in-law's work was steady. His boss, a kind Christian man, provided free accommodation to Hussein's parents – at first. It wasn't luxurious, but there was enough space to share with us.

Hussein's parents had one room and a kitchen. Our children Amal and Ahmed slept in the same room with their grandparents. There was also a room and a small kitchen for me and Amani, which eventually was shared with Hussein and the baby, Musa.

It was crowded, but it was a regular neighbourhood, not a squalid refugee camp. We were content, because we believed it was our home for just a short period, before we would be able to return to Syria.

Others fleeing war-torn areas of Syria fled over the border into Lebanon and crowded into rented places, or ended up in tent camps provided by the Lebanese government and the United Nations.

ISLAM AND CHRISTIANITY, IN SYRIA AND CANADA

In my culture, not all Muslim women wear traditional clothing and the headscarf, called "hijab." Many wear western-style clothing. Christians and Muslims, both men and women, are mostly indistinguishable from each other, and no one really cares about your religion.

In Syria, people have a general feeling about Christians, that they are nice people, they are honest, they will do things for you and not expect anything in return.

This was also true in Lebanon, when we lived there.

As I mentioned, there was a brief period when Hussein and I lived in Lebanon when we had just one child, Amal. Hussein's parents had remained in Lebanon from this early point, but Hussein and I returned to Syria. We did this because a conflict erupted between Israel and Lebanon in 2006. Although there was a ceasefire after only a month, there was a period when it seemed that all of Lebanon might not be a safe place. We chose to return to Syria. Eventually we returned to Lebanon, encouraged by his mother, as I have described.

In Lebanon, in the city of Zahlé, where his parents had settled, there were a lot of Christians. I think this is the reason that there was no bombing in the Zahlé area, when war broke out between Israel and Lebanon in 2006. People said it was because of the Christians.

The Israelis were bombing parts of Lebanon that they believed supported Arab-led insurrection in Palestine, so they bombed the more Arab-populated areas of Lebanon. So, what I knew about Christians was that they were nice people who did not get involved in wars.

In any event, this is how it came about that Hussein's parents got established in Lebanon, while we returned to Hussein's job and home in Syria.

Although I do not remember my father ever going to a mosque, he was a practicing Muslim in the sense of observing the holy month of Ramadan, living a Muslim life, celebrating Muslim holidays. My mother did regular prayers at home, five times each day, as observant Muslims do. I do not think my father did regular daily prayers.

All mosques are open all the time for prayers. Some people, especially men, will go to a nearby mosque for daily prayers, or may pray out of doors on a prayer rug in a public park. Not everyone is observant.

We did not know which of our neighbours were Sunni, like us, or Shia, and nobody seemed to care much about those matters. Of the two types, the Shia Muslims follow different disciples of the Prophet Muhammad, peace be upon him. They also pray to Ali, one of the chief leaders of their faith, asking him to mediate their prayers to Allah (God). This is different from Sunnis like us, who only pray directly to Allah.

Also, my Christian friends should note that many Muslims say the Arabic words for "peace be upon him," as I just did, when they mention the name of The Prophet, or even refer to his title. In written English, these words are sometimes shortened to PBUH. This is to show the highest level of respect.

I was raised by my mother to observe daily prayers. I do this now, even when I am at work. If the prayer time is close to my lunch break, I will wait and do my prayers at lunch. If we are entertaining, either in Syria or in Canada, sometimes I might slip away, make an excuse to leave the room, do my prayers and come back after a few minutes. Or I might wait until the guests leave.

I always want to be pure for the prayers, so if I use the washroom, I will purify myself with water, not only toilet paper. This is a necessary part of being pure for prayer, in my culture. I believe it may be different in other Muslim countries.

The requirement for purity also extends to being touched by a man, even accidentally, who is not a member of my immediate family. I might accidentally contact a customer, a man, when I hand him his change. If this happens, I will not be horrified, but I will find a way to purify myself before I can pray. I would do this by pouring water on myself.

I think it might be helpful for Canadians who are not Muslim to know how the Muslim faith affects daily life. It does not make us different, just helps us to maintain our awareness of Allah. There is a variety of ways of practicing the Muslim faith, just as I observe a lot of different ways for Christians to practice their faith.

I wear a hijab because that is the culture in which I was raised. It is how I feel comfortable. Also, of course, my husband has opinions about how I should look. In my culture, it isn't a good idea for a woman to adopt behaviours that make her seem like she is not a good and observant Muslim, because that reflects on her husband.

In Syria, as in Lebanon, I would leave the house and travel alone if I were going to a job, but otherwise it would not be normal for a woman to be travelling unaccompanied. Sometimes it might happen of necessity, but not as a choice. In Canada I can choose to do these things, and my daughters can also.

It is important to me to raise my sons to appreciate that women should have these freedoms. With sons, it may be harder to get those ideas across, whereas my daughters can see these things more easily.

My daughters see that I can get a driver's license, and can drive them around, even taking the children on a holiday when my husband has to work. I am showing them that there are no limits to what they can do in Canada.

In Canada, our friends include women who are teachers, administrators, the principal of a college, a lawyer and many others, who demonstrate the choices for girls in Canada.

Canada also provides a lot of opportunity for my sons. However, it is more difficult for them to see that a mother, even one who genuinely enjoys cooking, might want a bit of freedom from the never-ending task of preparing all the meals for an extended family.

When I lived in Lebanon, in the five years before coming to Canada, Hussein and I joined the household of his parents. Because his parents were already settled in Lebanon, we did not have to live in a crowded refugee camp.

His mother was not employed outside the home, but expected that I would care for my children and also cook for the entire household. The household was my own family of six, my mother and father-in-law, and all of Hussein's siblings who lived at home, which included a married brother, Mohamed, a single teen-aged brother, Mahmoud, and Hussein's single sister. She was employed outside the home.

It was a traditional large Arab-style house, with a shared kitchen, and separate rooms for each family or couple's sleeping area. Hussein and I had two rooms. The older children had one room. Hussein and I and baby Musa slept in the other.

My sister-in-law, Mohamed's wife, was of some help to me, but even so, a lot of the work fell to me. Even when I was caring for a baby, meals had to be ready when the men returned from their work. During this time, I also did sewing, making and selling clothes, to make extra money for the household. After three years of this, I was ready for a change, any change. I had no idea how much of a change Canada would be.

Similar to my family custom, Hussein was not raised to go to mosque on a weekly basis. It may be that In some Muslim-majority countries, the expectation is that all men will attend mosque. That was not true in my area of Syria, nor in the area of Lebanon in which we lived.

Sometimes the culture and the freedoms in Canada are confusing to me. I have a friend in Canada, a woman about my age. I assumed she was a Christian because of her clothes, which were not as modest as I would expect of a Muslim.

After I had known her for quite a while, I was surprised to discover that she was Muslim. She did not wear a hijab, but that is very common among Muslims, here as well as in Syria and Lebanon. The part that surprised me was that she did not hesitate to wear sleeveless tops, or show parts of her legs, in ways that, in Syria, would have been interpreted as immodest. In Canada, young Muslims can make their own rules about dress, and still be Muslim. My own daughters will have to figure this out.

DAILY LIFE IN LEBANON

We felt very comfortable in Lebanese society and culture, at first. Syrians did not have all the rights of Lebanese citizens, but there was work, and no hostility toward Syrians.

Hussein's father worked for a Christian businessman. Hussein also found car-repair work in a shop owned by a Christian man. At the beginning, I did not get any sense that people of different religions or different nationalities had difficulties with each other. This was also my experience in Syria.

Most men would take time to pray at the appropriate times during the day. Employers, even Christian employers, regularly accommodated their employees who required prayer times.

Mostly, when we lived in Zahlé, western styles like blue jeans were common among young women. When I saw a woman without a hijab, it was reasonable to assume she was Christian, but this was not always true. There may have been young Muslim women in Zahlé who chose not to cover their hair.

We were very fortunate that Hussein had skills that were in demand, and that he found work very quickly. If people had only farming or labouring skills, and were stuck in camps, they were much more desperate than we were. Still, taking care of the entire household was all I could handle.

Then, as the war got worse, more Syrians drifted into Lebanon. With them came the possibility that members of terrorist groups could be filling up the refugee camps, along with harmless farm families or city dwellers whose homes had been bombed. This situation made the Lebanese government anxious about the growing population of Syrian refugees, and less welcoming.

After we had been in Zahlé for about almost three years, there was a gradual shift in attitudes, both from the Lebanese government and from local people. Employers were less likely to hire Syrians, not knowing how to tell a peaceful migrant from a terrorist or a secret enemy.

Even if the Syrian employee was not a dangerous person, nobody wants to wonder if their employee could get arrested and dragged away without warning. Also, people in Lebanon began to blame Syrians for whatever might go wrong, whether it was crime or shortage of jobs or rising rents. More people were rude in public to those with Syrian accents.

HUSSEIN'S FAMILY FARM IS DESTROYED

Around this time, Hussein learned that his family's farm near Abu Adh Duhur, where he grew up, had been destroyed by the warring troops.

Members of Hussein's family had a big farm near Abu Adh Duhur, where many of his relatives lived. The climate was drier than near Aleppo, where my family could grow vegetables. Hussein's family could not grow tomatoes, peppers and other vegetables, but they had grain fields and olive groves. Irrigation makes anything possible, but the cost of trucks of water, or building wells and pipelines, made it impractical.

We will likely never know which army destroyed Hussein's family's home. All the buildings, crops and machinery were burned. All the animals (chickens, sheep) were gone.

Something I learned later is that warring armies first eat all the food in areas they overrun, including killing and eating all the livestock. Then burn or bulldoze everything to prevent enemies from returning to the area. The result is that the olive trees, which take many years to replace, are destroyed.

When the olive trees are gone, the farm is no longer a source of income. The olive trees also provide a food source (olives and oil). Without their olive groves, families can subsist on chickens and grain crops, if they can reclaim their land. Many choose not to. This is because their only hope of getting enough money to sustain a family, rebuild the farm, purchase new equipment, was the olive groves, and those are gone.

Nothing is as sad and discouraging for a farming family in Syria as the loss of olive groves. Many groves are very old, and have produced for many generations. Olives are seen as a gift from God, providing shade, food, beauty and income. The deliberate destruction of them is different from the slaughter of chickens or the burning of field crops because they cannot be replaced except over a generation.

Another challenge faced by people in Syria is that every family has lost at least one adult male, during the ten or more years of fighting. Young men have been killed as soldiers or as suspected rebels. For rural families, this means only old men, women and children remain to do the farm work.

In the city, it means that fewer working men have to support more people. But I am getting ahead of my story: Until later, we did not know that my family's farm and Hussein's would be completely destroyed. We did not know that Aleppo would come under some of the heaviest bombing of the war. At first, in Lebanon, we still cherished the hope of returning.

The time that our family lived in self-imposed exile in Lebanon stretched on. Altogether, our family lived in Lebanon for three years. Amal and Ahmed had already lived for two years with Hussein's parents, when Hussein and I joined them. The city, as I have mentioned, was called Zahlé. It is over an hour by car away from Beirut, which is on the Mediterranean coast. Going by bus almost doubles the time required.

A car trip from Abu Adh Duhur takes more than four hours, and even longer to get to Aleppo.

The fighting in Syria went on and on, requiring ever more sacrifices from the population. Schools remained closed, then there were shortages, then more men were required to fight, and so on. I believe that most people, like me, didn't know and didn't care what it was about, we just wanted it to stop, while there was still a "normal" life to which we could return.

APPLYING TO THE UNITED NATIONS

Hussein stayed in Abu Adh Duhur until his boss decided to close the business and leave. In Zahlé, Hussein found work at another welding shop, working for a man named Nazar. Nazar was also Syrian, but we did not know him until we moved to Lebanon. Nazar learned about the United Nations programs for refugees, and encouraged Hussein to apply to the UN, so that we could go to another country.

We did not do that right away, because we thought we would be able to go home. In addition, things for us were not too bad in Lebanon, at first.

Nazar was successful in arranging for his own family to go to Canada, a place we had never heard about, except from Nazar. "Come to Canada," he would urge Hussein, when he phoned from Canada.

Eventually we applied to the United Nations. The forms asked where we would like to go. We did not know what else to say, so we said we would like to go to Canada. The UN asked us for identity documents, but of course we had not been able to return to Syria to renew our identity papers. The UN people helped us to do that. They also provided an allowance for food, which was important as our household finances were getting more and more stretched.

NO JOY IN LEBANON

At first we were hopeful about the refugee process, because of Nazar's relatively swift success. Then months and years went by. With the increasing hostility toward Syrians, and high unemployment among Lebanese, Hussein's father's employment ended. With it, we lost the benefit of rent-free accommodation. We now needed everyone to bring in some income, if possible. I was able to do some sewing of clothes for other people. Hussein's mother had to look for work outside of the home. Hussein did not want me to work outside the home, because it hurt his pride if he could not look after his family. However, wages were low, especially for Syrian refugees living in Lebanon. Living costs were high.

As jobs for Syrians in Lebanon became scarce, and our combined household budget became desperately tight, the pressure on me to earn wages overcame Hussein's wish for me to stay home. I had to take a job on a vegetable farm, starting well before sun-up, until nine or ten in the morning.

The work day started around 3 am with travel out of the city to the farm, where the workers bent over in almost total darkness, cutting bundles of parsley and mint with sharp knives. It was difficult work, without breaks or light, except the light of the moon. The stems were tough and required strength to cut through them with the knife. I would return to the house exhausted, to begin my daytime tasks of caring for a baby and making meals for the household.

Although I enjoy preparing food, I did not find much joy in this phase of our lives in Lebanon. We had given up any expectation of hearing from the United Nations after so many weeks of waiting.

And then the phone call came.

My cell phone number was listed on the forms that we had completed at the UN office. One day, a man called from the Canadian consulate, on my cell phone, but his Lebanese accent was indecipherable to me. All I understood was that we were to come to an appointment at the Canadian consulate, the next morning at ten o'clock, if we were still interested in going to Canada. We were to bring our identity documents.

I panicked. I said, "I have to stay at home with my children. Can my husband come, instead?"

The person said, "Oh yes, just have him bring the identity documents for each member of the family who will be going with you."

"Going to where?" I wondered to myself.

Hussein was at work when the phone call came, so as soon as he came home, I told him that he would need to gather up all of our documents and take them to the Canadian consulate at ten the next day. Fortunately, the location of the consulate was only a short distance from where we lived in Zahlé.

Not surprisingly, Hussein had given up hope of ever hearing from the UN or from Canada, and thought this phone call must be a mistake. He went off to work as usual the next day, because it was important to have his income for the family.

At around 10 am, my phone rang. Again, it was the Canadians, wondering where Hussein was, because he seemed to be late for his appointment. I am not sure what I said, except that I promised he would be there very soon. I called Hussein. He was shocked. He rushed home from work, which was a ten-minute drive away, grabbed all the documents he could find, and hurried to the consulate.

Once this appointment was completed, it was amazing how quickly things happened. The first step was that we had to make a trip to Beirut. Hussein was told that we would need to go to Beirut to a place where we undergo medical exams. When I heard this, my hopes were dashed.

Going to Beirut for any reason was completely beyond our ability. The bus would take over two hours, and encounter several checkpoints along the way, where our papers would show us to be Syrians, meaning that we were not free to travel all over Lebanon. We would probably be removed from the bus and sent back to Zahlé.

When we expressed our misgivings, the consular staff were unconcerned. They had arranged a van to take our whole family to Beirut, to make sure we could complete the medical exams. They even arranged for us to stay in a hotel in Beirut so that we could be there in time for our early-morning medical appointments. This was all very exciting and dizzying. A hotel! I could not have imagined such a thing.

Only a few days after we got home from our trip to Beirut, we were again contacted by the Canadian consulate, advising us of our travel date.

I knew almost nothing about the place, Canada, that was our destination. Although I had a cell phone, I was unaware of the internet, or of the concept of searching on Google. I used my phone only to call people, using just the telephone function. Of course, I heard people talking about You-Tube and Google, but I did not know people who had data plans, and we did not have money to spend on that. If I had known how to use free services, such as at a library, I could have searched (in Arabic) for lots of information about Canada, its climate, geography and culture, but I did not know how to do this. I knew nothing except that Canadians speak English. I knew only one English word: "hello."

I admit being apprehensive -- I think anyone would be -- about going to live in a place where I would not understand anybody. In hindsight, had I known more of the climate and culture, I might have been in a complete panic. Perhaps a bit of ignorance is a good thing.

Hussein spoke by phone to people who had moved to Canada, like Nazar, so he heard some things about what life in Canada was like. Sometimes we heard from friends in Lebanon whose family members had moved to Germany, so we heard little bits of information about what life was like there.

Because my cell phone number was the one on our refugee application papers, I kept getting calls from people who tried to explain things, but I would usually give the phone to Hussein or get him to call them back. I had trouble with the accents of the people who called from the Canadian consulate, even though they spoke to me in Arabic.

A MYSTERIOUS VOICE

One of these mysterious voices, a man, was calling from Canada. He spoke with Hussein about two days before we were due to board the plane to come to Canada. Although the man called my cell phone, and spoke in Arabic, I struggled to understand him, and passed the phone to Hussein.

Later, I learned that the voice belonged to one of very few people at the two churches in Clarkson who spoke any Arabic. Obviously, his role was critical, particularly at the beginning of our time in Canada.

RAJAH MAKES CONTACT WITH ALIA AND HUSSEIN

A moment has arrived in this story for the Canadian volunteers to add their perspective. The first is the man with the mysterious voice, the man who contacted Alia by phone, Rajah. He is a small, white-haired man, a retired professor and a member of one of the sponsoring churches.

Rajah speaks:

Our church's refugee committee chair, Ruth, called me over to her house in late July, a few days before the Al Rmidain family was due to arrive. Ruth realized she would have difficulty conveying a few simple instructions to the parents without someone who could speak Arabic. We knew that Hussein had studied a bit of English, but he didn't seem to speak or understand much.

I consider that my Arabic is pretty rough, as it is not my mother tongue. I was born in Egypt, to Lebanese parents, and educated at an English school there. I learned French and Arabic as second and third languages. To make matters more difficult for Alia and Hussein, my Arabic is delivered with an Egyptian accent. Nonetheless, I made myself available to the refugee team in Clarkson.

My wife, Molly, also speaks a little Arabic. She is Scottish. We met when I was a university student in Glasgow, Scotland, where I studied law, then accounting. This was decades ago, of course. Later, as young parents, Molly and I lived in Lebanon. It is a lovely country, and we enjoyed our time there.

Lebanon is a country of great beauty, with warm and friendly people. The current residents are the heirs of one of the world's ancient and proud civilizations. Molly wanted to raise our small children there, but I was concerned about what was happening to the country, as well as to surrounding nations. Minority and majority religions and populations were increasingly coming into conflict.

When the country of Lebanon was carved out of Syria, at the end of the first World War, a careful balance was struck between the Christians and the majority Alawite Muslims. The constitution established that the president would always be an Alawite, and the next strongest role in government would always be a Christian.

This careful balancing of power kept the country peaceful and stable for a long time. However, over time, the balance shifted. Cracks were creeping into an otherwise stable society. I saw this happening decades ago, and persuaded my wife that Lebanon would not be an ideal place to raise our children. We moved to Canada.

Now, with the influx into Lebanon of large numbers of refugees from Syria during the civil war, the cracks are widening. Resentment and suspicion widen these gaps: the Lebanese worry that members of militant groups have infiltrated with the peace-seeking refugees.

The Syrian civil war has severely strained relations between religious groups in Lebanon, as well as in Syria. Suspicions grew, corruption increased. The Lebanese government slowly tightened the screws on Syrians, finally preventing them from working and supporting their families.

Increasingly, the Syrian refugees became dependent on international aid, and desperate to leave. This was the milieu in which Hussein and Alia found themselves.

I was delighted to be of assistance to the refugee committee at our church. Molly and I had already helped to prepare the kitchen, with supplies of suitable Middle-eastern groceries, and we wanted to do more. I accepted Ruth's challenge to try to communicate with Hussein, to tell him what to expect upon arrival in Canada.

I was also eager to make the trip to the airport, to help with interpretation, and be among the first to greet our new Syrian friends.

I made the call. I did what I could to assure Hussein that an apartment would be waiting for them, and that they would be met at the airport.

Figure 1:   English and Arabic welcome sign.

Figure 2:   Molly, Ruth and Rajah preparing the kitchen for arrival day.

Figure 3: Master bedroom ready for arrival day.

Figure 4: Heather, Rev. Jim, Nancy and Jeanine at the airport, August 5, 2016.

Figure 5: In the back row Heather Nancy, Ken, Jim, Rajah, with Amal, Hussein, Ahmed, Musa, Alia, and Amina in the foreground, at the aireport.

Figure 6: Hussein begins to line up the skewers, once the coals are just right. He brings his own Syrian-style barbeque to gatherings.

Figure7: Hussien and Ken carving pumpkins.

Figure 8: Alia, Hussein and the children express their gratitude
to their United Church friends.

Figure 9:   Rev. Jim barbeques in Canadian style, while Alia looks on.

Figure 10:   Amina and her friend Cam at Cam's grandparent's cottage.

Figure II: Most of the fish were tiny and did not require a net, and then, this surprise!

Figure 12: Ahmed's cub ceremony day.

Figure 13: Hussein and Ruth with the children at the
Terra Cotta Maple Sugar Festival.

Figure 14: Ken teaches snowmen-building.

Figure 15: Amal and Ahmed at Tim and Jeanine's pool.

Figure 16: Alia in one of her favorite places in Canada.

Figure 17: Ruth, Carol, Alia and Sue after Alia's presentation at the IODE.

PART TWO

PART TWO

READINESS

A committee of volunteers from two churches divided up the chores that they expected the newly-arrived family would need. These volunteers were to become Alia's and Hussein's friends, but also their teachers, drivers and supporters. Rajah and Molly were team members. Each of the church congregations could call on three or four other Arabic-speaking helpers as needed but on the first day, the arrival day, translation fell to Rajah.

When the support team of volunteers first met, Ruth and Jeanine were chosen as co-leaders, one from each of the two largest congregations.

Nancy, a retired medical technologist, became the coordinator of drivers, making sure the family got to all of their appointments. Others worked at outfitting the kitchen, painting, finding furniture, hanging curtains, gathering books and toys, and keeping track of donations.

Team members were brimming with excitement over the impending arrival of strangers who were known only by their names and ages.

Nancy, the volunteer in charge of scheduling the other volunteers to provide rides, visited the multicultural services in Mississauga to get help to design a welcome sign in Arabic characters. One of the hand-lettered Arabic signs was added to the church's lawn sign. The welcoming party took the other sign to the airport on arrival day. Nancy hoped that Alia and Hussein would see their names on the sign, in Arabic, and connect with their team at the airport.

AT THE AIRPORT ON ARRIVAL DAY

Nancy speaks:

It was a last-minute idea: I had volunteered to make a welcome sign to hold up at the airport. We knew they could scarcely speak or read English, except maybe Hussein had a tiny bit of English. I carefully copied out their names in Arabic characters on a big sheet of poster board. Not knowing anything about Arabic script, I had to check with Rajah to make sure it I hadn't made any mistakes.

On the big day, we all herded to the airport, in several vehicles. We did not know how much luggage could come with six people. As much as they could drag or carry, we assumed. Heather had a child-seat for Musa, who was about two and a half, and a booster for Amani. The two older ones would not need boosters.

My husband Ken and I had a van to take luggage. Ruth, Jeanine and Rev. Jim had room for luggage in their vehicles, too, if required.

It was sort of festive at the airport. We were not the only "welcome" party waiting for the same flight. Tension built as the crowd in the waiting area stood around for what seemed like hours – actually, it *was* hours. We chatted with the other sponsoring groups, and made new friends.

There was a set of double doors where people emerged from the baggage-claim area, after they had cleared customs. Every time those doors slid open, dozens of us looked in that direction, stood on tiptoes to see – to see what? We didn't even know what our people looked like! All we knew, each time the doors opened, was whether another planeload of people was streaming through. We had no way to know if it was *our* planeload or not. Each delay and disappointment ramped up the suspense.

There were seven of us: Rajah was there to translate, plus our co-leaders, Jeanine and Ruth. Rev. Jim from the United Church also drove, as well as Heather, Ken and me. We wanted to have lots of people to help with the children and luggage. And, well, some of us just wanted to be there. It was exciting.

We had been fund-raising for months, and had easily reached our target. Then there was the furnishing of the apartment. The most amazing things happened. Clearview Church, which wasn't formally part of our three-church group, had a quilting group. They gave us quilts for each child's bed. I think they did this for several sponsoring groups. It was truly a community effort.

Rajah and Molly, because they had lived in Lebanon, were extremely helpful in equipping the kitchen. They knew what groceries and supplies would be familiar. They knew, for example, where to get halal meat to put in the freezer and fridge. The rest of us had never needed to shop for halal meats! Like anything else, it's easy once you know, so Ken and I took the parents shopping many times, after that first day. The first time, though, it was Rajah and Molly to the rescue!

Small groups of people kept coming through the doors into the "welcome" area of the airport. Each time a young-ish couple with children appeared, we held up our sign and waited for a response. Finally, there it was. A man looked over at us, grinned from ear to ear and directed his wife to look at our sign. They had found us!

We were probably also grinning like circus clowns, unable to do anything else, with no language to greet them. Rajah stepped in to make introductions, and to try to explain that we were going to divide up the luggage and people into several vehicles. I'm sure none of it sunk in with Alia and Hussein, but who cared about that? We just wanted to get a few pictures and hit the road home. I'm sure they, too, just wanted to get out of the airport.

After taking pictures, Heather got Alia and all the children in her car, and started out. Ken and I were right behind her, with some of the luggage. In Heather's car, there was no one to interpret. We left Rajah translating for Hussein and the rest, so Alia got no explanation about how long a car trip to expect, or where we were going. We did not realize what a brave step this was for her.

It took about twenty-five long minutes, from the airport parking to the church parking lot.

THE DRIVE FROM THE AIRPORT

Heather is a retired director of patient care at a hospital in Mississauga. She participated in setting up the apartment, getting it furnished and equipped for the family.

Heather:

It was SO frustrating, being in the car with Alia and wanting to ask a million questions. She had a few of her own, I have no doubt. Later I learned that she thought we were taking them to a hotel. There was simply no way to explain that our church had an unused apartment on the second floor, and that it had been fully equipped as a temporary home.

All of the volunteers had agreed that, although it was inside the church building, it was a good temporary solution for housing the family. We had allowed for the possibility that a Muslim family might be uncomfortable living in the church, and might want to move fairly soon. That isn't what happened, though!

Alia could not say more than "Hello" to me, of course, so she looked around silently, or spoke softly to the children in Arabic, while I drove. Later, she told me that her initial impression of the Canadian landscape changed minute by minute during that twenty- or twenty-five-minute car ride.

I concede that the Toronto airport and its surrounding highways are drab, perhaps even ugly. However, as we left the highway and got closer to our destination, she saw trees, lush lawns, flower beds, and beautiful homes. Canada seemed to be just as it had been described to her.

When we drove up to the church it was mid-afternoon. The church's sign had a line in Arabic saying "welcome." Alia couldn't read the English part of the sign, so she didn't know she was entering a church. I led her and the children through a side entrance, along a corridor and up the long narrow staircase. The door at the top of the stairs opened into their new apartment.

She just stood for moment, staring in amazement, then walked in and began looking around. I will never forget the astonishment on her face. The children followed her, hesitant but enchanted by what they saw.

In the turmoil at the airport, we volunteers had not given much thought to explaining things to Alia before separating her and the children from Hussein and the interpreter, Rajah. I had been in the apartment with her for a minute or two when I could see that she was agitated, and no longer taking anything in.

"Hussein? Hussein?" she called, into the empty air, and looked at me with a wide-eyed look of growing panic.

I had no way to explain to her that his car was perhaps five or ten minutes behind us, due to the need to load up the luggage. There are no hand-gestures for such a situation. Getting separated from him would be her greatest fear; how could we have failed to think of that?

After a few long minutes, we heard voices, then the thumping of footsteps on the stairs. Hussein, Rajah and a few of the other volunteers entered the apartment. Immense relief brightened Alia's face. The crisis had passed. She could breathe again. She took some time, then, to absorb her surroundings.

I was inwardly quite proud of what we had done to prepare every room, every cupboard, for them. All I could do was smile, nodding my encouragement, and watch while she studied it all. Gradually she figured out that it was a home, not a hotel, and that it was all for them. I wouldn't have missed that moment for anything.

DEAD, DRY GRASS. CAN THIS BE CANADA, AT LAST?

A lia:

When our departure day came, we made our way to the airport in Beirut to begin our journey. We had only what we could carry in our suitcases. Airports and air travel were completely new to us, of course, but the novelty ceased to have much appeal after many hours in the air. The trip seemed endless.

Our first sight of Canada consisted of the brown, parched grass of August around the runways of the Toronto airport, viewed through the airplane's tiny windows. The rest of it, as far as I could see, was a sterile, industrial wasteland – like the area around the Beirut airport, but endless. Stories that we had heard of a lush and beautiful country seemed to be inaccurate.

I struggled not to be disappointed by this first impression, as we had no way to return, even if Canada proved to be ugly and desolate.

After the plane had been on the ground in Toronto for what seemed like an eternity, we were allowed to step off the airplane. We trudged, exhausted, down seemingly endless, bleak, corridors, carrying the younger children. We were surrounded by other weary and confused people.

The airport was a terrifying place for me. I had never been in an airport before we went to Beirut to board the plane. It was evident from the conversations around us on the plane that we were not the only refugees on our flight.

I was too tired to worry about what would happen next. Hussein believed that somebody would meet us. Why he believed this, I was not sure.

I could not read any of the signs in the airport, of course. I held onto Musa, who was then about two and a half years old, and followed Hussein. My stomach was clenched with anxiety. We would progress, then be held up by a line-up. After a wait, we would show someone our papers, then proceed to another place. Line up again. Produce papers. Wait again.

The waiting and processing at the airport dragged on and on. It is so hard on families with children, to wait in line for your turn, to sit while paperwork is filled in or reviewed.

A woman from Pakistan took pity on us and helped us to know where to go, where to wait and wait, and what might happen next. Finally, the very busy Arabic interpreter came and sat with us, because there were papers we had to sign. They had to be read to us in Arabic first. I don't remember what we signed. It was all a blur.

We had been on the ground for three hours before we were shown to the area where we could look for our suitcases. All this time, my stomach had been in a knot. We were all feeling scared and unhappy, but there was no possibility of changing our minds. And of course we were all hungry, which made it more challenging to keep the children calm.

Finally, hauling our luggage, and encouraging the children, we reached a set of large doors leading to an area that was open to the public.

We had finally reached the arrivals area! Those doors were like the entrance to Canada.

Until that moment, I felt fear at every stage in the process, believing that we could be refused admission to Canada at any point. Then, as we emerged through those doors, from the almost-silent baggage area into a wall of voices and conversations, and seeing the throngs of strangers, I was still anxious. Inwardly I said, "We have made it to Canada, but what do we do now?"

Moments later, Hussein called to me over the heads of the children. He had found somebody. I followed his gaze, and saw a sign with our name spelled in Arabic.

That sign! Some of the volunteers had prepared a sign with Arabic lettering and Canadian flag stickers. Without it, I do not know how we would ever have identified our new friends in the huge crowd.

Having seen the sign, my whole body was flooded with relief. Clutching the children and dragging our luggage, we still had to swim through a sea of people to get to the group of smiling, friendly people holding the sign. But that sign changed everything. I told myself, "We are going to be okay."

ARRIVAL IN CLARKSON:

N**ancy:**

So many wonderful things happened that were unplanned! For example, the afternoon that Heather, Rev. Jim, Ken and I arrived at the church with the exhausted Syrian family, a group called Pedalheads were using the church grounds to give kids instruction in bicycle safety. During the summer, Pedalheads rented church space inside and outside, for a sort of bicycle day-camp. Outside, they used the lawn and one of the church's parking areas.

This group had read the English version of the welcome message on the church sign, and knew what was happening. When Heather's car, then Jim's and ours rolled into the parking area, the Pedalheads instructors stopped what they were doing, got all the kids to dismount and line up in a row. Then the counsellors and kids stood and clapped while Heather led Alia and the children into the Sunday school wing of the church. Rajah, Ruth, Jeanine and Hussein were behind us in traffic somewhere, so they missed this part. It was very moving, a wonderful gesture, by children to children.

A day or so later, the Pedalheads instructors offered the Syrian children a free week of bicycle camp. Ahmed had already learned to ride in Lebanon, but it was new for the girls, so this was just ideal. Clarkson Road

Presbyterian Church had rounded up suitable bikes for all of the children, and off they went to their first summer camp activity in Canada!

The three older kids had a wonderful time at Pedalheads. As an added bonus, one of the teen-aged Pedalheads instructors was bilingual in French, and so could explain in a way that Amal and Ahmed could understand, with their grade-school French from Lebanon. At this point none of the children had a single word of English. That didn't last long, though!

After that, it was lovely to walk up to the church entrance and see the children's bikes lined up in the bike rack outside – a cheery reminder that an active family was living in our church building.

I MUST LEARN ENGLISH, SOMEHOW

A lia:

In August 2016, just days after we had moved into the apartment in the church, Nancy brought me the test for English skills, so that the ESL (English as a Second Language) school in Mississauga could place me in the proper group. Then another new friend, Jeanine, came to the apartment with a young Egyptian woman from Christ Church who spoke Arabic. Her name was Christine. Together, we completed some paperwork that was needed to enroll me in the ESL school.

Hussein started his English classes in our second week in Canada, getting rides from the volunteers. He would come home with homework, and was excited about learning and meeting other refugees.

I was not sure how I could ever learn English. My new Canadian friends were encouraging me to go to school, but what would little Musa do while I went to school? And I couldn't even think about that in August. Amal, Ahmed and Amani would start school in September. Maybe after that, I could figure out what to do.

Fortunately, the older children would all be going to the school that was right next to the church where we lived. No drivers, no buses, just walking across the parking lot! That was one of the main reasons that we were satisfied to live in the church. Also, it made it very easy for all of our new friends to visit us frequently.

The elementary school beside the church had a French language programme. We did not enroll our children in that programme, because we needed them to learn English first, even though the older ones had learned a bit of French in Lebanon. However, there were times, at the very beginning, when the French-speaking teachers were the only ones who could make Amal and Ahmed understand. Our younger daughter, Amani, who knew no French, did not have this advantage, but she learned English quickly.

It was a great relief when the children started school, but then there was homework for them to do! My Canadian friends had thought of how the children would need help with their studies. I was completely unable to help with the children's homework, and Hussein was busy doing his own homework. So, every evening, a volunteer came to tutor the children. They were just wonderful. I wasn't able to learn along with the children, as I had hoped, because Musa wanted my attention.

My new friends worked on getting a place for Musa in the daycare where the ESL classes were held. It took a little while, after the older children had started classes, and then, suddenly, the daycare was able to take Musa. I was supposed to get ready to leave Musa and spend the day in class!

I had no idea what to expect. Hussein was enjoying his classes, and making good progress. In Lebanon, he had learned to read English a little. I think this helped him, as he started his ESL classes. I, on the other hand, could not read or speak English at all. Even the English alphabet was strange to me. I was happy for Hussein that he was gaining English skills, but very worried that I would not be able to learn.

In early October, Nancy drove Musa and me to the first class, the class for absolute beginners. By this point, Nancy had been a frequent visitor in our home. Musa was reasonably comfortable with her, but, in his short life, he had never spent any time away from me. How could this work?

When we arrived for the class, Nancy went off with Musa to get him settled in the area for children. Of course, he burst into tears when he figured out that I was going somewhere else. This was very hard for me. Nancy reassured me, and sent me off to my class. She got Musa settled with the teachers, although he continued his crying. Then she stayed nearby.

When I arrived at my class, I cried, too. I worried about Musa. I didn't understand anything. There was no one to whom I could pour out my anxiety, in Arabic. All I could do was cry.

Poor Nancy! She found me in tears at the end of the class, and was very concerned and mothering. Apparently Musa had eventually stopped crying, perhaps from exhaustion. I felt terrible for him.

Nancy didn't know why I was crying, and was very worried. She took me and Musa to our home at the end of the class. Soon after, she came back later with Jeanine and with the young Egyptian woman, Christine, as interpreter. They sent everyone else out of the room so that I could speak, in Arabic, just to those three women.

I think they were relieved to know that my burst of tears was about my lack of English, and about Musa, because they were sure that time would take care of Musa's anxiety. If there was another sort of problem, such as a health worry, or bad news from back home, they would not have had a solution.

For the first few weeks of my English classes I made very slow progress. I worried about Musa, who continued to wail loudly every single day that I left him in the daycare. This was very hard for me, and made concentration difficult. He also prevented me from focusing on homework until he was in bed at night, and by then I was too tired.

What I did not realize was that, all the time in daycare that Musa was wailing, or sobbing quietly, or silently sulking in a corner, he was gradually starting to understand the teachers and other children. He did not speak for weeks. Then, suddenly, he was ready to speak.

He did not say anything in English until sometime in December, but when he started, he said whole sentences, not just one word or two. As well as learning English at daycare, he heard a lot of English spoken at our house in the evenings. The older children sat around the table and spoke English with their homework coach. Sam or one of the other volunteers came frequently to go over Hussein's homework with him, and practice speaking English. Musa was absorbing English gradually from all of our visitors.

At about the same time, his attitude to daycare changed. He surprised Nancy, early in January.

The school resumed on a frosty January morning, after closing for the Christmas break in late December. It was Nancy's turn to pick up Hussein, Musa and myself, to take us to school. The ESL school was in a storefront, in a small shopping plaza. When Nancy parked in front of the ESL school, the first one out of the car was Musa. He bolted to the door, hit the pad to make the door open automatically, and dashed inside with a yell, "Bye, Nancy."

Expecting tears, Nancy was amazed.

It made a huge difference to me when Musa adjusted to ESL. He was learning English so quickly that he began correcting the rest of us, at home. He would also answer our visitors' questions in English, while the rest of us were still struggling to understand the question.

One day when Pastor Jim visited, Musa was sitting on the floor, pretending to prepare some food, using Playdough. Jim asked him what he was making. I started to translate Jim's question to Arabic for Musa, but before I could do it, Musa said "Chicken," without even looking up from his task. Pastor Jim was very impressed.

It became easier for me to focus on my English homework, once Musa was happier in the daycare. Instead of climbing into my lap and interrupting my attempts to do homework, he became more comfortable talking to the visitors, or playing on my cell phone, or playing by himself.

Still, I was not learning very quickly, and found the English classes frustrating, until the volunteers organized coaching for me. Hussein and the older children already had homework coaches, but it would not have worked for me to have coaches until Musa settled down, because he needed my constant attention for the first few weeks.

At the beginning, my coaches worked with me, at home, on whatever had been studied in the class that day. We practiced talking, just saying the new words. Small steps. Later, my various teachers helped me with grammar. Very soon, thanks to all of my tutors, I was learning ahead of my classmates, and getting ahead of the teacher.

Most mothers with children would not have any opportunity to use or practice English from the end of one class until the beginning of the next class, but I was coached for an hour, four evenings per week. It was enormously helpful.

Hussein did not get the amount of coaching that I got, and really did not need it as much, because he could make himself understood in English. He was far ahead of me in English fluency, after just a few weeks of study.

He had set a goal of reaching Level Four in ESL in one year, and then looking for work. He achieved this. I was very proud of him.

He could also leave the house in the evening and find people, men, of course, to talk to, either in Arabic or English. He was placed in a more advanced class, Level Three, at the ESL school. At first, I could not even use the Arabic-to-English phone app without help, because I could not read the English-equivalent words.

When I first began my English classes, I had no words, and could barely make myself understood except with the phone app. I was uncomfortable with the idea of having coaches, if I could barely communicate with them.

Once I had a few words in English, and the coaches began visiting me to help with homework, they were very helpful. The time my volunteers invested in me quickly paid off, for me. Even so, it took two years of ESL, combined with coaching, for me to get close to Hussein's level of confidence.

At first, Musa was jealous of the time I spent with my conversation coaches, and kept trying to get my attention. Gradually he learned to entertain himself.

Also, one of my coaches, Lorna, would bring her grandson, Alex, who was just a little older than Musa. Alex would play with Musa in the basement until bedtime. This allowed me to spend more time on my homework, with Lorna's help.

HOW TO BECOME A LANGUAGE COACH

L orna:

It happened by accident. My work requires a lot of travel, so I did not think I was in a good situation to volunteer for the refugee committee. Then, one Sunday at church, I had a chat with my friend Carol. She mentioned how excited she was about coaching Alia in conversational English on Wednesday evenings. She explained how long Alia had waited for a daycare spot to open up, and that, after a few weeks of ESL classes, she needed coaches to help with her homework.

I had met Alia and her family some three months earlier, on their first Sunday morning in Canada. The family lived upstairs in the church and attended the service to listen to the music and practice listening to English.

Everyone knew who they were, the very minute they showed up on Sunday morning. Alia was the only woman wearing a hijab. I'm sure she didn't know who I was: just one more, in a sea of unfamiliar faces.

Anyway, I asked to tag along with Carol on her next visit with Alia. That first Wednesday evening was so much fun that I suggested that I could be Carol's alternate, to spend part of the evening with Alia when Carol was busy.

Does "fun" seem like an odd choice of words? Well, first, there was Musa, climbing into Alia's lap and trying to get her attention away from Carol. When that didn't work, he tried to grab Alia's phone, which we were using for the Arabic to English phone app. My grandson is just a bit older than Musa, so I enjoyed this immensely.

Then there were the hilariously awkward pronouncements from the translation program, as it tried to turn her questions into English. Some made Carol and me giggle, which left Alia wondering why her question, sensible in Arabic, was amusing in English. We were helpless to explain. Then a few Arabic translations of our remarks gave her a puzzled look, and she saw that the phone app was charmingly inadequate. We carried on, because what else could we do?

We discovered that the best use of the app was for translating individual words.

When Alia understood that I wanted to come back with Carol, she disagreed. Alia proposed another idea. She said to me, "I want you to come on Mondays, and Carol on Wednesdays." The phone app was perfectly clear, this time, so I began coming every Monday evening.

At the beginning, I would get home from work, grab a bite to eat on-the-run, and show up at Alia and Hussein's apartment around 7 pm. Frequently, when I arrived, there was a male volunteer coaching Hussein and yet another volunteer, a woman, sitting at the dining room table with the children, supervising their homework. It was an atmosphere of quiet chaos.

The apartment was cozy. Although designed to house the church's custodian, it had not been recently used except as extra meeting space. There were two bedrooms and a sort of large, windowless room that was also needed as a bedroom.

Previous to the family's arrival, the entire space had been set up with folding tables and chairs. Our congregation held work-bees in that space, getting ready for the church's Christmas bazaar, and storing our craft supplies there.

The first time I visited the family, I followed Carol up the narrow staircase from the main level of the church. She knocked and we were warmly welcomed. I had not been up those stairs in many months, and was astonished to see the place furnished for a family. All I could think of was "Where are all the pine cones and glue guns?"

It was never intended as long-term accommodation for the family, but it worked. Although barely adequate for six of them, Alia told me it was so much better than the space they had in Lebanon that they were very comfortable. Delighted, in fact.

The volunteers had furnished the bedrooms, living room and kitchen with some used and some new furniture, and enough pots, pans, utensils and dishes that Alia had to buy very little to make it her own space.

Right next door to the church was an elementary school, which the three older children attended. No buses, no drivers needed! In addition, due to the school's French program, there were teachers who could speak to Amal and Ahmed in French, when English words failed them.

The church apartment, as I said, was very cozy, no, more like "cramped," when all of the family, plus volunteers, were applying themselves to homework. From the dining room there would be steady conversation among the three school-aged children and their tutor. Most conversation would be in English, but sometimes the children would converse in Arabic, if one understood before the others.

Occasionally the conversation with the tutor might be in French, which the older ones had learned in school in Lebanon. Meanwhile, I would be sitting close to Alia in one corner of the kitchen, while another volunteer sat with Hussein and worked on his homework in the "living room." It had a loveseat and chairs, but was really the same space as the dining room.

For the first year that I did this, my grandson Alex and his mom, my daughter, were living at my house. Alex, being just a couple of years older than Musa, was happy to come with me, and play with Musa. Had it not been for Alex, Musa would have made it very difficult for Alia to concentrate.

With all these English-speakers coming into his home, and at the day care while Alia took classes, Musa learned English at an amazing rate.

Later on, Musa was able to entertain himself, playing games on Alia's cell phone.

Alia always offered tea, coffee and snacks to the volunteers, as if all of us were her lifelong friends, and not strangers volunteering to help. I tried to always take something with me. Sometimes I took flowers, and often I took baked goods.

The men on the committee were coaching Hussein. This had the added benefit of giving him some Canadian friends. Cultural barriers prevented him from being friends with any of the women volunteers, at the beginning.

I wondered if Hussein would be uncomfortable with my style, which is sometimes teasing, sarcastic and not as respectful as he might have expected. He was a little reserved at first. Within a few months, though, Hussein had overcome the training of his youth: he even gave and accepted warm hugs from everybody, even me. That was before COVID, of course.

After my first few visits as a conversation coach, Alia invited me to come earlier and have dinner with the family. It was obvious that she loved to cook, and also wanted to be able to show hospitality to the volunteers. It was no problem for me to go directly to Alia and Hussein's apartment after my work day, often bringing my grandson Alex, stay for dinner, and then work through her homework from ESL class.

After beginning this new routine, I had a sense that she was putting on a fancy dinner because I was there. One of her many showy dishes involves small eggplants and zucchinis stuffed with a lamb and rice mixture. It must take hours to assemble. That didn't seem quite right, so I made it clear that I could eat what the family normally ate. Her food was always good, so what did it matter?

I am pretty stubborn, so Alia eventually relented. After that, I was served simpler fare, still delicious.

I am fairly sure that the routine I observed was repeated every evening, with a different set of volunteers. Because I wasn't a member of the original refugee support committee, I didn't meet all the others until the family moved into their new place. And what a party that was!

Their first house party happened after a bit more than a year in the church's apartment. Hussein and Alia had found a townhouse, and furnished it with some additional tables, cabinets and sofas acquired at our church's annual spring sale.

As soon as they were settled, Alia and Hussein invited everybody they knew in Canada to celebrate moving to their new place.

They were now at ground level. Guests were crammed in. There were carpets, sofas, chairs, footstools, a coffee table, and a well-worn dining room suite. People perched or squeezed into every space, including a few on the floor. And so much food!

Alia had cooked wonderful Syrian dishes in large quantities, as if the volunteers were not bringing anything, but of course they all did. You could hardly move, even when her children and my grandson disappeared to the basement.

One event had made the move possible: Hussein had found work at a truck repair shop. He usually got home at seven or so. Dinner usually waited for his arrival, but often Alia fed the children first.

Hussein had made very good progress in English, too, putting in long hours of study. After almost a year, he was eager to get out and start earning to support the family. He was justifiably proud of his ability to use his car mechanic skills in Canada. The job, offered to him by an immigrant Canadian, an Italian man, I think, was in Georgetown, a drive that took at least forty-five minutes at the end of the day.

Almost immediately he proved his worth at the shop and began putting in long hours, sometimes working weekends as well. This put an end to his language classes and coaching. He had reached Level Four, which is more than adequate for most day-to-day purposes, and more than many new immigrants achieve in their first year.

It took Alia quite a bit longer to pass Level Four. Eventually she did, and proceeded joyfully to Level Five. Having had very limited schooling in Syria, she believed she was not smart. When I observed, early in our acquaintance, that her lovely children all seemed very intelligent, she smiled and modestly waved at Hussein, as if to suggest they had inherited that trait from him.

I emphatically shook my head and pointed back at her. She offered me a look of surprise, but I insisted. She was beginning to have confidence. She could succeed, just as he had. She just needed to believe in herself.

She was a very engaging student, always ready to laugh. I spoke a handful of Arabic words, not enough to really help. I tried to answer her questions in fractured Arabic and English, with lots of hand gestures and occasional absurd suggestions spoken by the phone app. We typically laughed and talked quietly for hours, through clearing away the meals, and seeing the children off to bed after their volunteer tutors went home. Finally, when it was almost ten o'clock, I would realize it was time to go. I thought she must be exhausted, because I was.

When Alia began to look for work, she had completed Level Five at her ESL classes, and was very proud of her accomplishment. She wanted to proceed to Level Six, where she knew that her difficulties in reading would create a major challenge. Orally, she had become amazingly fluent, telling jokes in English and laughing appropriately when others told funny stories. But there was another barrier to going on in ESL: she wanted to contribute to family finances, and to make herself more financially independent.

There was a Dollarama store within a very short walk from her home. Alia had become acquainted with the manager in the most natural way. She was a frequent shopper, and would try out her English wherever she went. When a part-time job became available, the manager accepted her, based on her friendly manner and English fluency. Of course, Alia could provide no references.

A lack of Canadian employment history can be an enormous barrier for newcomers. Alia was aware of this, and was most appreciative of the manager who took a chance on her.

The day she got the job, she happily spread the news to all of her Canadian friends, and of course we were delighted, too. I'm sure her feet barely touched the ground for days.

At first the work in the store was part-time only, with sporadic hours and a rather chaotic schedule. This caused Alia to miss being home for some meals. More duties fell to her older daughter, Amal, who made sure the others got off to school if Alia had to open the store in the morning. When Alia worked afternoons, she left food for Amal to reheat for the evening meal.

Alia's manager began to rely on her, and increased her hours and responsibilities. While this generated more income for the household, it cut in on what Alia viewed as her duty to her family. It also reduced the time that she had available for English coaching. When she had an evening off, she was frequently preparing food that Amal could reheat the next day, or catching up on other tasks like laundry. My visits diminished in frequency, and I'm pretty sure the same was true for Alia's other language coaches.

When the woman who hired Alia was ready to offer her almost full-time hours, Alia could no longer get to ESL classes at all, even though she had a car by this time and could drive to class. Homework was no longer critical. I continued to visit when I could, especially when she began to work her way through the materials for the citizenship exam. She showed me the material she had to learn for the exam and asked me some questions. I joked that I would have to study for such a test, too, although I have lived in Canada since birth. I wished her luck and laughed. However, both she and Hussein were very determined to take this step at the earliest opportunity. Months later, after much diligent study, and some coaching, both she and Hussein passed.

Some of Alia's teachers and coaches had training or experience in education, whereas I was just winging it. One coach, Elisabeth, had taught ESL and is multilingual. Another, Sue, had been a teacher and elementary school principal. Ruth, one of the children's homework tutors, had taught high school, and another tutor was a teacher as well. Jeanine, gosh, I don't know how many degrees she has.

However, when I compare notes with the others, it was not about educational style or the substance of the curriculum that contributed to Alia's success. It was her thirst for knowledge and her joy in the progress she was making.

Alia was the ideal adult student. She was driven and tireless. More than that, she was fun! She quickly became a friend to each of her coaches.

My sessions with her covered so much more than what her ESL homework required. We laughed a lot, I remember that. We spoke of our families, things that made us happy or sad, things she missed about Syria (not much!) and whether she would ever go back. She was very emphatic on that point. No. Just "no." She loved Canada for the opportunities it provided to her and to her children, particularly her daughters.

MY FIRST JOB IN CANADA

A lia:

As Lorna has described, I secured a job at Dollarama, once my English was good enough to wait on customers and answer their questions. I had become friends with the manager. By the time I was ready to look for work, we had moved to a townhouse very close to Dollarama. The manager recognized me as a frequent shopper. I am so grateful to her that she took a chance on me.

I did not have full-time hours at first, so I was still able to attend some ESL classes. Gradually the manager expanded my hours and my responsibilities. I was proud and delighted, but of course this put an end to my further ESL classes. I could still have visits with my coaches, when I didn't have evening work. After so many months, they had all become friends.

By this point, I could enjoy a chat with each of them about their families, their careers, favourite recipes, or any topic. I felt like we were enlarging our friendships, but still affording me the opportunity to learn new things about English expressions and words.

Serving customers in English at Dollarama was terrifying at first: I needed to learn patience and to trust myself. For example, if a customer asked where to find Christmas wrapping paper, I would understand, and direct them to the correct aisle. But sometimes, they would ask, using a word that I had never heard, such as spatula or sieve. I would ask, "Where do you use it?" or "What is it used for?" They would say, "In the kitchen." Since we have only one aisle with kitchen equipment, my problem was solved, and so was the customer's. Bit by bit, I gained confidence, and my manager could tell.

I find that most customers are kind and patient, and also express gratitude when they get help. For the others, I just assume that they have worse problems in their life than I have, and I try not to let their bad manners affect my day.

GROCERIES IN CANADA

A lia:

There was an Arabic grocery store in Mississauga called Adonis. Almost every week, at first, Ruth drove us to Adonis for groceries. Sometimes Jeanine would help me to write out a grocery list to give Sam or one of the other volunteers. I can shop in a regular Canadian grocery store, if I have to, but it is so much easier to have an Arab grocer, where I do not have to struggle to understand what the products are, and where I can find the varieties of vegetables I need for Syrian dishes.

The types of cucumbers and zucchini, the type of tomato paste that I use, the noodles I prefer, these are all available in Mississauga, typically at Arab or Chinese or Korean grocery stores. My Canadian friends often express surprise when I serve them. I believe I am introducing the Canadians, gradually, to more interesting and delicious foods, foods that are available in this country but unknown to them! I think I am succeeding, because they keep asking me about my plan to open a Syrian restaurant.

I still long for a time when I might be able to manage my own restaurant business, to share my favourite dishes with Syrian-Canadians, as well as with other Canadians, but this is not the right time. I want to get my children well settled and finished their education before I take on such an all-consuming job as managing a restaurant, or even cooking in someone else's restaurant. Someday I will do this. Canada is a place where dreams come true, from what I have seen so far.

HUSSEIN GETS ADVICE

Alia:

Sam, an Arabic-speaking member of the Presbyterian church, was among the first who came to the apartment for one hour each night to help Hussein with his English. He was very kind and helpful. He was generous with his time, and in other ways – and not only to us: he is regarded as a leader in the Syrian community in Clarkson, providing advice and assistance to all who ask.

As I have mentioned, he disagreed with the committee's plan for our family. He wanted Hussein to get a job right away.

Some of our other new friends, including Rajah and Molly, who spoke Arabic, strongly disagreed with Sam. They wanted Hussein to accept the churches' support, just for one year of concentrated study. They explained that the Canadian government sponsorship scheme required the support committee, our friends, to provide for our needs for the first year. The aim of this scheme was to make language classes a priority. They said Hussein would never have the time to focus on English if he didn't do it now.

Hussein agreed. He set a goal of studying as hard as he could for one year, before looking for work.

Sam was worried that we would be those people who look for every hand-out, and become lazy immigrants. At the time, I did not understand why Sam felt so strongly about this, and disagreed with the others. I was troubled by this disagreement, because we really appreciated Sam.

At the end of our first year, Hussein was indeed looking for work, and found a job, but we were not yet ready to move out of the church's apartment. We needed to save for our first rent, and we were reluctant to change the children to a different school, so we waited until there was a place available in the same school area. After a year and three months, we did move to our own place, but the delay may have irritated Sam!

Later, I came to understand. Sam had probably seen people who will abuse any situation. Even Hussein says that other new-comers in his ESL classes told him about free money, "welfare," that the government pays you for just staying home, not working. I have met those people, too. Immigrant women ask me why I want to have a job. But I am getting ahead of myself. I'll tell you about that later.

Hussein was adamant that he was not at all interested in taking government money for an extended period, and would have preferred to take none at all. However, he saw the wisdom of working on his language skills, to improve his employment prospects. He could have found welding work right away, but he chose to study first. His goal was to get to a level of fluency useful in many workplaces, and he reached it in under a year. It was hard for him to accept financial help for that first year, but it was the right decision for him and for our family.

Language was also a critically important step toward getting Canadian citizenship. That was one of our goals, almost from the moment our plane landed.

WE ATTEND CHURCH

A lia:

People ask why we go to churches, if we are Muslims. We do not want to become Christians, but I believe my children will understand Canada better if they understand the culture of a mostly-Christian country. By attending, we learned about the United Church and the Presbyterian Church. We learned about Christmas, Easter, and all the activities that take place at a church.

I find that I can worship God when I am in a place where other people gather to worship God. The details don't matter to me.

The volunteers from the two main churches asked if we wanted to get a ride to mosque. My husband said that would not be necessary, as he had seen what Islam did to Syria, and he did not think he needed to go to mosque here.

In truth, he did not attend mosque regularly in Syria, so this was not a big change. In the parts of Syria where I lived, and where Hussein had grown up, it was not customary for all the men to attend Friday prayers at a mosque.

Women did not go to mosque, generally. That is my experience.

On Sunday mornings, when we first arrived, we did not have anything else planned. All we had to do to attend the church was to get dressed and walk downstairs. We attended Christ Church at 9 o'clock, most Sunday mornings. We also attended Clarkson Road Presbyterian Church almost every Sunday. It took only a few minutes to walk from the early service at the United Church to the 10:30 service at the Presbyterian church.

In the years that we have been in Canada, we have been asked to speak to both the United and the Presbyterian churches in Clarkson, so that those who are not part of our volunteer support team can know something about our family. We have been happy to express our gratitude for the help we have received. We are independent now, but we remain grateful for the help and friendliness that marked our early days in Canada.

At Christ Church, the United Church where we lived in the upstairs apartment, the church's pastor, Rev. Jim, made sure that my husband got a printed copy of the sermon before the service began each Sunday. Hussein asked Jim to do this.

I could not read English at all, at the beginning, but Hussein could. He could follow along as Jim was speaking. Hussein would circle any words he did not understand, and talk to Jim about them later. In this way Hussein improved his reading. It also helped us to understand what the Christians were learning, and what they thought about God and about other things.

Hussein was far ahead of me in reading and writing English, having studied some English in Lebanon. I had not studied English at all, and had a lot more difficulty learning the English alphabet. Even now, reading does not come easily. At that time, I did not try to read Jim's sermons. But we could participate in Sunday worship as much as we chose to.

The early service at the United Church had a band, with two guitars, a drummer, singers and a piano. Sometimes there were other instruments as well. The words to the songs were on a large screen at the front of the church, so the children (who were learning to read English much faster than I was) could read and sing along. Soon, they knew some of the songs.

The music leader of the band was a tall, friendly man named Jason. He could sing wonderfully. He also played piano, flute, trumpet and maybe some other things that I have forgotten. Jason ran a summer activity at the church called Band Camp. Our older children signed up in 2017. They learned to play recorders, to read some music, to ring chimes and hand-bells, and to play a few notes on band instruments like clarinets and horns. Ahmed also took the guitar class.

This was the first opportunity that my children had to play instruments and make music in a band. The three older children attended all day, at the church. In addition to band and singing classes, they also learned to make cookies and to do some crafts. Stories from the Christian Bible were taught. At the end of two weeks, there was a concert for parents and friends. Each child at the camp performed, some in twos and threes, and then all of them in a big, noisy band. Our family thoroughly enjoyed participating in Band Camp.

We also signed up our three older children for the Christmas plays at both churches in each of our first three years. At the United church, the children practiced every Saturday morning in December, then put on the play with costumes, songs and music on a Sunday evening. In 2016, the play was a story about travellers from outer space landing on earth and hearing about Christmas. Ahmed, our second child, played the part of a robot. It was a good part for him because he wasn't ready to learn a lot of spoken parts in English, after only a few months of learning English in school.

Later, Ahmed's cub pack troop was asked to help to lead the annual "Scout Sunday" service, held in the usual time for church. All the cubs, scouts, beavers, and other groups for children wore their uniforms to church.

Although the cub and scout groups met at Christ Church, only a few of the children and families actually belonged to that church. When it was time to choose someone to read a lesson from the Bible, the leaders chose Ahmed, maybe because he was part of the congregation. By this time he could speak English pretty well, but it was the first time he had read in front of an audience. He did a very good job. Nobody seemed to mind that we were not Christian. We were very proud of Ahmed.

Our children also joined a children's choir called Tempus4Us. The practices for this choir were at Clarkson Road Presbyterian Church. Our friend Ruth drove the children so that they could enjoy this activity and meet other children.

Ruth stayed during the practices, and sang with them, to help the children learn the music. She also helped them to understand the words they were singing. This helped with their reading and their knowledge of English. Ruth ended up being a general choir assistant.

This choir sometimes sang in church and also put on two concerts each year, in spring and fall. Of course we were proud to be in the audience with all the other parents!

In the spring of 2017, the Tempus4Us choir put on a concert for parents and others. The theme was to recognize Canada's 150th birthday. As well as singing, the director asked some of the children what Canada meant to them.

Our daughter Amal was one of the speakers, although she had only been learning English for about eight months at that time. She said that, in Canada, she would be allowed to go to school for as long as she wanted to, and that she could become anything she wanted to be. I cried tears of happiness when I heard her say this. It was my dream for her – it is still my dream for her.

PUBLIC TRANSIT AND MY DRIVER'S LICENSE

A lia:

I became very close to our friend Nancy, a retired lab technician, whose family immigrated to Canada from Japan. Her husband, Ken, was also from a Japanese-Canadian family. Unlike most of the other volunteers, Ken and Nancy knew about belonging to a visible minority, and they knew about settling into a new country, even though both of them were born in Canada.

Nancy was a key member of the refugee team because she arranged rides for us, especially to our ESL school. Although I wanted to be independent, I had to accept help, at first. The rides that we got from volunteers made a big difference in my life.

I could get to the ESL school on public transit, from our apartment at the church, but every trip required at least two bus routes, and a stroller for Musa, who of course had to come with me. This was time-consuming and exhausting, even after I got to know the city and the bus routes a bit.

In addition, I could only run errands with Musa while his brother and sisters were in school, so I had to be sure to allow enough time to get home. Getting a ride from one of Nancy's many volunteers, both for ESL classes and for shopping errands, was very helpful.

Later, after living in the church for a year and three months, we moved to our townhouse, which was right on a major bus route. After that, getting to places by public transit was quite a bit easier. I became less dependent on drivers. We still remained close to Nancy and Ken, who became like grandparents to our children.

The day Hussein got his Ontario driver's license brought huge excitement to our family. Even though he had a driver's license from Lebanon, there seemed to be so many steps. Finally he got his license. Shortly afterward, he found work, and then needed to buy a car. Going to his work by bus would have taken more than two hours each way. By car, it was less than half of that time.

Finally, with Hussein's purchase of a car, we were gaining independent from our reliance on the volunteers to drive us. He worked long hours, so I still needed to use public transit some of the time. However, on his days off, we could do things and go places, even visit friends in Hamilton, or drive to a park near Lake Ontario, without involving the volunteers.

For my part, I had observed with interest that a great many of our volunteer drivers were women. Even before I had enough English to learn about their lives, whether they were married, widowed or single, I saw that these women did not take along any accompanying male member of the family, when they used a car. At first, I did not imagine myself ever being like them, but slowly the idea grew. However, studying for the driver's test seemed like an insurmountable barrier.

After several months of English language study, I was becoming more fluent in spoken English, but reading was still very difficult. Two of the volunteers, Al and Jeanine, came on alternate nights to study the driver handbook with me, patiently reading in English and discussing the diagrams and pictures with me, until I understood.

Then I discovered that I could take the test in the Arabic language! What a relief! Since I knew the material in the handbook, and the test was in my language, I had no trouble at all. I passed and got my G1 license. I think I messaged or phoned everybody I knew within the first hour. I was absolutely thrilled!

In Ontario, this meant that I still needed to spend a lot of hours driving under the supervision of a licensed driver, before I could drive on my own. Again, my friends came through, and took me out for short drives as often as they could. The biggest adventure came when our family visited at Jim's and Ann's cottage, again. I was able to do practice-driving on the country roads, with Jim or Ann, or their daughter-in-law Danielle, as my coaches.

It seemed to take forever to become confident at the wheel of a car. After much practice, in 2019, I took my road test and passed. That day, like the day I got my first job, will be etched in my memory forever. Those are some of the events that made me a changed person.

WAITING FOR THE LIGHT
TO CHANGE

J eanine:

In addition to falling into a role as one of the coordinators of the volunteer team, I signed on as a driver. Ruth, the coordinator from Clarkson Road Presbyterian Church, was also a driver. Our roles put us in frequent contact with the family. Both Ruth and I became very close to the entire family.

I cannot say enough good things about Polycultural Services, an amazing organization in Mississauga that helps get immigrants settled. Among many services, they have translators and case managers available. We, I mean the committee members and volunteers, used Polycultural's offices for accurate translating, such as when the application for Hussein's drivers' license needed to be filled out. I remain deeply grateful for the wonderfully helpful staff at Polycultural Services.

Hussein's license application was approved, and soon he was interested in acquiring a car.

In the early days we used a lot of hand gestures to communicate, to supplement the English-to-Arabic phone app, which could be quirky. Obvious mistakes in translation added a great deal of amusement to the exercise.

However, it was also frustrating when Alia could understand the questions, but didn't have enough English to answer without relying on the phone app.

One day I was driving Alia to an appointment, soon after Hussein had completed the arrangements to get his driver's license. I asked Alia if she was interested in getting a driver's license also. She shook her head from side to side, waving her hands in front of her, in a way that was very dismissive of the idea. I wanted to ask her why, but for her to adequately explain, I sensed that we needed the phone app to interpret, so I decided we could discuss the subject later.

Soon after my question to her, we were stopped at a red light at one of Mississauga's multi-lane intersections. In the car to our right were two young women, both wearing hijabs, as Alia was. The driver, while watching for the light to change, was engaged in a lively conversation with her passenger. There was nobody else in the car.

I noticed that these two had caught Alia's attention. Until that moment, I do not think she had noticed that hijab-wearing, Muslim women drive cars in Canada. It had just not crossed her mind. She knew that all of the women volunteers drove themselves to her house to tutor her or the children, and drove the family to appointments. But these Christian volunteers were not like her, or so she thought.

When the light changed from red to green, it was almost like a similar shift had happened in Alia's head.

I caught a sidelong glimpse of the look on her face. It was the opposite of the dismissive gesture she had given me just a few moments earlier. Instead, it was a yes-I-can look of surprise. After that, it was just a matter of time before Alia was asking for help with the driver handbook.

COOKING WITH MY CANADIAN FRIENDS

A lia:

When it was Carol's turn as my language coach, we talked a lot about cooking, and sometimes we cooked. We used Google to translate the names of ingredients.

Carol always wanted to know the exact recipe I was using. That made an interesting challenge for me. Cooking that way, by measuring, is not my style at all. It was useful to stop and figure out the measurements, and how to say them in English.

Carol said that Al, her husband, doesn't follow a recipe either. He is like me, learning the basic ingredients that are needed, and making adjustments if he doesn't have enough, or if he wants to add a different flavour, or if a mixture seems too thick, or too runny. Carol said she never cooked that way! I was surprised.

Learning about Canadian food by eating in Canadian homes was a great adventure for my family. I also loved to cook for my Canadian friends. Some had travelled and were familiar with Syrian dishes, and some were cautious.

Eating with Molly and Rajah was the most relaxing, because we could all speak Arabic. Molly's grasp of Arabic was a bit like my grasp of English: she sometimes struggled to keep up, and Rajah's accent remained a problem for me, but we managed. We were in their home several times, and in the homes of many other new friends.

REV. JIM MAKES MAKLOUBA

A lia:

Rev. Jim invited our family to his house for a meal a few weeks after our arrival, before we could speak more than a few words. Hussein used Google Translate or another phone app through dinner, to answer Jim's questions. On that occasion, Jim cooked a Palestinian dish called maklouba. This is a one-pot meal with rice, chicken, cauliflower and onion.

Jim and his wife, Ann, had invited a friend, Manal, an immigrant from Israel, who spoke Arabic as well as fluent English. Manal worked at the legal clinic where Ann was the director, and did a lot of interpreting there. She helped with our conversation, as we were helping Jim to prepare the meal.

The idea of maklouba is that everything cooks in one pot, and when it is ready, you invert the pot onto a large platter. It makes a mound of chicken pieces and cauliflower pieces, with lots of flavourful rice.

Jim had made a large batch. He was about to turn the pot over when Manal cautioned that his platter was not going to hold it all. She was right. Just in time, Jim found the biggest baking tray that he had, and used that instead. The hot food flowed right to the edges. It would have been all over the kitchen counter if Manal had not spoken up at the right time. We all enjoyed a delicious dinner.

Jim also served some interesting pickles. I think that every country has some form of pickles, but still there are surprising differences.

Our friend Rev. Jim likes to cook with Indian spices, making curries and Indian pickles. We like these things too. I like to talk about cooking with Rev. Jim.

I think Jim and Ann ate leftover maklouba for several days, and Manal took some home as well.

OUR FIRST THANKSGIVING

A^{lia:}

In October, not long after the maklouba dinner made by Jim, we were invited to have Thanksgiving Dinner at Jeanine and Tim's house. Rev. Jim and Ann, Ruth, Carol and Al were also there. With our four children, there were thirteen people around the table.

In my culture, we generally do not sit around a table, in chairs. It is much more common, at large gatherings, to use a large, open room, with carpet, and with low furniture around the outside of the room. Food dishes are spread out on a table-cloth on the floor, in the centre. People help themselves, or they may be served by the women, as they sit around the room and hold the plates in their lap.

We quickly adjusted to Canadian-style group meals, with everyone crowding around a table.

Some foods on the Thanksgiving table were familiar. Turkey, for example, is commonly consumed in many middle-eastern countries. On the other hand, pumpkin pie was a curiosity. We eat some types of squash, such as zucchini, but we do not make dessert with the orange meat of squashes like pumpkins.

Nancy and Ken could not join us, but they delivered an apple pie to Jeanine, before the party started. The children love apple pie, and were happy that there was an alternative to the pumpkin pie!

SYRIAN BARBEQUE: THE BEST KIND

A lia:

Hussein loves Syrian barbeque, so this is something that we try to prepare for our Canadian friends. It allows Hussein to share his cooking skills with the other men.

A Syrian barbeque must be done with charcoal, so it takes more care and preparation than turning on a propane grill. Hussein is a firm believer in the superior flavour of meat grilled over charcoal, as opposed to propane. Hussein's barbeque is a rectangular metal box with folding legs, and no lid. It can be set up in the backyard of our townhouse, or in a park, or at a friend's backyard or cottage. When it is cool and the coals are emptied out, it goes easily into the back of a car.

While he is nurturing the coals, by fanning vigorously, I typically teach the Canadians how to put pieces of marinated chicken and vegetables onto skewers, or how to shape a mixture of ground lamb and herbs into a long sausage-like kebab, on the flat skewers. Then, when Hussein is satisfied that the coals are ready, we line up a long row of skewers over the coals.

Canadians do not use flat, metal skewers, so their kebabs roll around instead of cooking evenly. They should learn from Syrians!

I use a lot of pita bread. My children have learned to live on Canadian bread, and to eat hamburgers and hot dogs, but to me, every meal from morning to evening requires pita.

All of our friends are thoughtful about buying halal meat when we eat together. To me, it doesn't matter much about turkey and chicken being halal, but eating pork is not acceptable in my culture. We also prefer beef and lamb that has been butchered in the halal fashion. This means that it has been killed swiftly and humanely, with the blood drained in an approved way, and with a prayer in Arabic. I think this is not greatly different from how Kosher meat is butchered, except for the prayers.

I have been happy to find many grocery stores in Clarkson that have lots of halal meats. I want to be able to observe the requirements of my faith while still enjoying a good social time with my Canadian friends, who are almost all Christians.

When Hussein is almost finished cooking the meat on the barbeque, I bring platters lined with pita bread. The bread is to absorb juices, but I also use a pita in my hand as a sort of oven-mitt, to help slide the food off the hot skewers. More pitas are used as towels to cover the top of the platter to keep the food warm while we take it to the table. When everyone has eaten, we use the remaining pita to roll up the leftover pieces of chicken kabab, or lamb kabab. I slide the roll of pita and meat pieces into a plastic bag, to be warmed for the next meal.

So, as you can see, I use pita bread for many purposes in the kitchen! I would be lost without it.

One of the things I miss about Syria and Lebanon is the ready source of fresh pita bread: In my country, there would be a vendor on almost every street corner with a small cart and a very high stack of large, flat pita for sale, from very early in the morning. Some families would bake their own pita, but many would buy a daily supply, as it is quite inexpensive. I can buy it in bags in Canadian grocery stores but I still miss the sight and the aroma of piles of fresh pitas on the street vendors' carts.

THINGS THAT ARE SIMPLY NOT POSSIBLE IN SYRIA

A lia:

Some things that my family has done in Canada are not possible in Syria because of the culture, and other things because of the climate.

For example, when we had been in Canada only four months and we were still struggling with English, our friends invited us to go sledding. It happened to be Christmas Day, when normally all of our Canadian friends are having a meal with family, but these friends were having their family celebration on the following day. They had the afternoon free. They invited us to go sledding on a hill near their house. A layer of fresh snow lay on the ground.

They had plastic sleds for us to use. One sled was long enough to allow four people to go down the hill at once. At first just the children went down the hill, with our host, while Hussein took video and pictures of them. Then Hussein and I also went down the hill, with our friends taking pictures.

Our whole family was also invited to learn to skate. Nancy's husband, Ken, took the children to a place where they could learn, and spent a lot of time fastening the children's skates, as well as his own. A generous family had purchased new skates in the right sizes for each child, in our first winter in Canada.

I am not sure if skating is something I could ever enjoy, but the children were thrilled to have a chance to learn. Hussein and I were grateful to Ken for the time he took with them, just as if they were his own grandchildren.

Amina told me all about it, and described how Ken skated around the frozen pathways with them while the children struggled to keep their balance. She told Nancy and me, "I am not afraid of falling because Ken will catch me." I am amazed that, somehow, Ken always managed to be in the right place. It was clear that Amina believed in him completely.

In warmer weather, we also experienced backyard swimming pools for the first time. Our friends Tim and Jeanine had a backyard pool. They had no children, only two cats. Tim and Jeanine became very fond of our children, treating them like their own. Jeanine taught our children to play in the water, and then to swim with lifejackets.

Our friend Ruth helped us to enroll the older children in swimming lessons in 2017, our first full summer in Canada. Later on, the youngest, Musa, was also able to take swimming lessons.

Ruth also drove them to their lessons, as it was too far to walk. I encouraged the children to take advantage of every opportunity that was offered, and they did!

The swimming lessons turned out to be very useful, when we were invited to visit a cottage. Jim, the minister of the church where we lived, has a small cottage on a lake near the town of Parry Sound. When Jim and Ann invited us to go there, the children were already accustomed to swimming. Hussein had learned how to swim in Syria.

It is normal for Syrian men to learn to swim, but less common that women would have such opportunities. I had never been in the water of a pool, lake or river.

Our hosts advised me that I would need a costume for swimming. I think Ann wanted to make sure I had no excuse for staying dry. By this time, I had watched my children swimming in the backyard pools of some of our friends, and I was becoming curious.

My daughters went shopping with me for a swimming outfit. For me, this meant a modest bathing outfit which included a long-sleeved swimming dress and leggings that covered me to the ankle. Lots of Muslim women, like me, do not feel comfortable swimming in more revealing clothing. Modest swimming costumes are available in Canadian stores if you know where to look. I made sure that I was ready for swimming.

I was very hesitant, at first. Just immersing myself in water was a new feeling. The lake water was much colder than I expected, although it was mid-August. My children encouraged me, otherwise I would not have believed that I would ever get comfortable in the lake water. I was standing in water that came just past my waist, and was wearing a life jacket, so I was in no danger at all, but that is not how it felt to me!

The water did feel a little warmer, as I stood in the lake, trying to gather my courage to get completely wet. The next step was to trust the life jacket to hold me up. That was almost too much. I did it because I saw my children doing it, thrashing around in the water, playing, and jumping off a diving raft. I knew I had to try.

All of us wore water-shoes because there were some stones and sticks on the bottom of the lake. I was covered from the soles of my feet to my hair, which was covered by my head-scarf, my hijab. That is how I feel most comfortable.

Thus prepared, I was determined to do what the children were doing. With much encouragement, I finally crouched down, very slowly, in waist-deep water until the lifejacket was holding me up. The sensation of weightlessness was completely unnerving. It took a few minutes to adjust, while I clutched the life jacket.

I think I may have been giggling, but this was just my way of suppressing a feeling of panic. Next, I had to release my grip on the lifejacket and try moving my arms. So far, so good. Then, I took my feet off the bottom and kicked my feet behind me, the same as the children were doing. I was swimming! Yes! I was wearing a life jacket, but now I could join the children in splashing merrily around in the lake.

It might be hard for a person raised in Canada to understand how exciting this was to me! Even though I needed a life jacket, this type of "swimming" was a major milestone for me.

Only a day or two later, on a hot afternoon, our host, Jim, announced that he was going to swim to the island that was about two hundred meters away. It is a tiny island, uninhabited, with several large trees and a small clearing in the middle for a tent site. My children spent one exciting night in tents on this island!

Jim invited all the adults and children to join in the island swim. His own children and grandchildren were swimming, the younger one with a life jacket and the older one paddling a kayak in case anyone needed to rest by grabbing onto the boat.

Some people swam, some had long floating devices called "pool noodles" and some, like me, wore life jackets. In a group of about nine or ten, we slowly crossed the calm lake. We stood up on slippery rocks when we got to the island, laughing as we lost our balance. Then we came back.

It wasn't a great distance, but the feeling of accomplishment for me was as if I had crossed Lake Ontario.

Let's

PADDLING, FISHING

A lia:

While we were at the cottage, I experienced boats for the first time. Our hosts had several varieties of kayak, boats that could be operated by one person, or by two people, using double-ended paddles.

On our first day of boating, there was almost no wind, so the water was very calm. First everyone got a life jacket. Then they sent us out, children and adults, one or two in each boat, with only a short period of instruction to make sure we could get back. Then they let us learn.

All of the children were thrilled to have the independence to use a pedal-boat, or to be alone in a kayak. I took a two-person kayak. My younger son, Musa, sat in the front seat, without a paddle, while I learned how to steer the boat.

There was also a canoe, but I preferred the type of paddling with the double-ended paddle because the steering is easier to learn.

Going to Jim's and Ann's cottage for a few days each summer has become a highlight of our year. Since both Hussein and I have been working, it has become more complicated to get time off together. Sometimes he cannot leave his work for several days in a row, so I have taken the children to the lake by myself. Driving a van by myself, and taking my children to a vacation place, these are opportunities that did not exist for me in Syria.

I am so glad that I am able to get a few days off to go to the lake every summer.

Once I went in the spring, to help Ann and her daughter-in-law Danielle get the cottage ready for summer. They told me that there can be a lot of mess, if mice get inside during the winter, but we must have been lucky. There wasn't much work, so we just had a pleasant trip with a few chores. Such a car trip, with no children or husbands, could not have happened in Lebanon, even if we were invited to a summer cabin.

When I spend a few days at this lake, I take any opportunity to be alone in a kayak, just paddling a short distance from shore or even going around the island. Sometimes, when I am in the middle of the calm lake on a sunny day, I like to telephone my friends in Mississauga, or even Facetime with friends back home in Syrian or Lebanon, and show them that I am far from shore.

I also learned fishing. Our friends have lots of fishing equipment, some of it very old and repaired, but good for a lot of children and adults to go fishing at once.

The older children like to be in their own small boats, or to fish from the diving raft, but I like to sit in the small motor boat, and help Musa. He is not as good with the fishing equipment as he thinks he is, at age seven.

After many tries, and many lost worms, everyone in the fishing party landed a fish – yes, even I caught a small fish. Everyone had the satisfaction of having a photo of our catch. Then we gently removed the fish from the hook and threw it back into the water.

Most of the fish that we caught were rock bass, and were not much bigger than my hand. Musa claimed that we were just catching the same fish over and over again. I don't think he was right, but it didn't matter. It was still exciting to feel the tug of something on the end of the fishing line.

Once or twice the children reeled in a fish so large that the adults had to use a net to get it out of the water. Then they used tools to free the fish from the hook, instead of doing it by hand. Those ones make the best pictures and stories. As we always do, Hussein and I sent photos of the children and their fish to their grandparents and relatives back home, to show what new things they are learning in Canada.

On my fourth trip to Jim and Ann's cottage, I finally learned to swim without my life jacket. Of course, like anything else, this is frightening to learn. I wish I had overcome my fear earlier, but my teachers were patient. So far, I cannot swim very far, or make my arms and legs work together, but I know I will learn.

OUR FRIENDS IN CANADA

A lia:

Another time our friend Jeanine invited us to her vacation place. She and Tim had moved to Alberta by this time, and we missed them terribly. They had become like real family, while they lived in Mississauga. A few months after they had moved away, Jeanine came back to Ontario so that she could visit family members, but stayed at her vacation place in Blue Mountain, near Collingwood, Ontario. She rented a place nearby where we could stay, and all of us enjoyed the area.

I have treasured these opportunities for vacation time and new experiences for the children, Hussein and myself. It was not our family custom, either in Syria or in Lebanon to travel. Being invited to vacation places is something that I have learned to love about Canada and Canadians.

I am proud and happy to say that, in Canada, I have a lot of friends. This is so important to me because I have left behind my mother and all my family members. Cell phones make distances seem less, but it is also important to have friends nearby.

In addition to the Canadians that I know from two churches, some of my Canadian friends are Arabic-speaking friends from a variety of countries. These include my neighbours, and classmates from language classes. They share with me the experience of being newcomers in a strange place, and learning a new language.

Many of my neighbours are new immigrants, not from Arab countries. We communicate with each other using our only common language, which is our newly-acquired English skills. This handicap is not important, because we share the common experience of being far from family.

I also have many Canadian friends who have included us with their families and the activities that they do for relaxation. They already have lots of friends and family, so there is no need for them to add a Syrian family, my family, to their social circle. I am so glad to know these people! They have enriched my life and enriched the lives of my children in so many ways.

My children have had many opportunities to discover what Canadian children do on special days. At Hallowe'en, the children have carved pumpkins, and have dressed up in costumes. At Christmas, they have assembled ginger-bread houses and stuck candies on with icing. In the spring, they visited a maple sugar bush. At Canada Day festivals and other occasions, they have tried out climbing walls, water parks and other activities.

I wanted to describe how much I appreciate my life in Canada, and to tell my friends how much Canada has changed me. I got this opportunity in the Spring of 2019, in a way that I did not expect.

LET'S DO THIS!

C arol:

It was magical to watch Alia's confidence in English grow to the point where she agreed to tell her story in public, after only three years in Canada. The opportunity came through my friend Sue, who was Alia's language coach on Thursdays. Sue is a retired elementary school principal. She was taking a turn as president of the Oakville chapter of a women's service organization, the I.O.D.E., when she had the idea of inviting Alia as a guest speaker. Each month a guest would address the twenty or thirty women on some topic of interest.

When Sue proposed the idea to me, I was skeptical. I tried to picture myself, if I were learning a new language, standing in front of a crowd of strangers, pouring out my story. Not on your life! It took me years to develop my confidence speaking in front of a group in my first language!

The next thing I knew, Alia had agreed to do it, apparently because Sue told her, "Don't worry about a thing. You can do it. Carol and I will help you."

"If Alia's up for this, of course I will help! Her story is amazing, so let's do this," I said to myself.

Initially, Alia began to have doubts about communicating her story to a crowd. She had been in Canada less than three years. Her conversational

English was quite good, but she had never spoken to a group, in any language. Here, she would face a large group of older women. There would be no immigrants among them, as far as she knew, and certainly no uneducated Muslim women. Why would they be interested in her or in what she had to say?

Sue and I assured her that they would be interested. We promised to make it as easy as we could. All she had to do was tell her story, just as she had told it to many of her Canadian friends. I would join her in front of the audience and prompt her in a question-and-answer format, so she did not need to be nervous. I would also have slides on a power-point, summarizing what she was going to say. With the slides on a screen, the audience would be sure to understand and she would have a visual guide to help her stay on track.

We brainstormed topics and rehearsed at Alia's home over several visits, so that Sue and I would know what she intended to say. Eventually, our game-plan emerged: I would use the bullet points on the slides as a basis for questions to prompt her, in a dialogue format. This would keep the story flowing in case she got nervous. I also wrote out some of her responses on cue cards as a back-up in case she lost her train of thought at any point.

I need not have worried.

I assumed that Alia would be able to work with visual aids, as I would, if I were doing a presentation. As we progressed with our rehearsals, it became apparent that she needed only verbal cues. Beyond this, she simply organized her thoughts in her mind.

On the big day, I said a silent prayer for everything to go well for Alia. Having gotten her into this situation, I felt partly responsible for her comfort level and success. I felt this burden particularly when she first began.

Once she had been introduced, there was only a brief period of nervousness on Alia's part. I asked one, or maybe two questions from my list, to put her at ease, and within minutes, I felt that burden lift as she took off, like a runaway horse.

Along with everyone else in the room, I was carried along on her story. It was like being airborne. She kept her audience spellbound for about forty minutes. She could easily have kept going if there hadn't been a specific time allotment for the presentation.

Perhaps it was the sense of having their undivided attention that gave her the energy to do what she did. The I.O.D.E. women are accustomed to experienced and polished speakers addressing their meetings, but were struck by the fluency and passionate delivery of the young, radiant hijabed woman who stood before them.

Alia spoke passionately of the fear of the unknown in leaving her homes, first Syria, then Lebanon. Then she shifted into the joy of discovery, once she had settled in Canada. Her life here was exploding with possibilities, not only for herself, but for her daughters. Her husband and sons would thrive, and adapt, but her message for a gathering of women was that the Canadian experience was empowering, liberating, and exhilarating for her as a woman.

She paused at one point to reflect that, if things ever improved and it were possible to go back to Syria, she would simply not be able to return. She could not return to being the person that she was, in her old life.

Coming to Canada had changed her into a new person, a woman who could achieve something outside the home if she chose, a woman who could move freely in her community, who could learn, and whose daughters could have careers.

These sentiments were so passionately expressed that the listeners could hear the sincerity, the enthusiasm in her voice. While I was there to facilitate the flow of Alia's story, I also became a witness to what was happening in the room. At one point I looked out at the audience, and could see by the expressions on their faces that they were hanging on her every word. What power she commanded, speaking fluently, from the heart and without hesitation! She spoke in full paragraphs, having no need of prompts. She was confident, she was emphatic, she was riveting. And she seemed to know it. This girl was on fire!

I had the feeling that parents have when they let go of their child's bicycle seat, and watch the child pedal off down the sidewalk for the first time. Like that child, she was carried away by the thrill of her first public-speaking engagement, no longer needing even the reassurance of my presence. As with a parent, my heart was bursting with relief and pride!

Alia was triumphant when she reached the end, knowing that she had conquered her fears, and accomplished what she had set out to do. Even so, she was not quite prepared for the adulation that the I.O.D.E. members showered on her after her presentation.

Even today, when I remember that day almost three years ago, I'm amazed at this transformative moment in Alia's journey. I had been among the first to sit with her for evening conversations. We had struggled to connect with each other, using the Arabic-to-English phone app, when she had fewer than two dozen English words at her command. How far she had come!

Patiently, courageously, over many weeks and months, we had shared personal information. She knew, almost three years on, that I had retired from a professional career, as had several of her other conversation tutors. She knew that my husband and I had each been previously married. Divorce was a confusing feature of Canadian society. It was not part of her previous experience. Naturally, she was curious to discover that the apparently perfect lives of her Canadian friends were not always flawless.

We had become friends through cooking together, through sharing the joys and frustrations of settling her children in their schools, and through all the exciting achievements. For me, all of these experiences had bonded us, so that I was heavily invested in my dear friend's life story. I was proud of her accomplishments in learning English, and, frankly, amazed at her seemingly effortless delivery of her story.

Those in her audience at the I.O.D.E. spoke to their friends and neighbours about Alia. Requests were received for more presentations. She did speak, at the Presbyterian Church, and at the United Church. On those occasions, the congregations wanted to hear from the whole family, so Alia was not in the spotlight. Hussein and each of the children had a few moments to speak about adapting to Canada. Alia's presentation was brief on these occasions, to accommodate Hussein and the children. I heard afterwards that her fluency in English and her confidence astonished those who had not been in touch with the family's progress since their much-anticipated arrival three years before.

One of Alia's and Hussein's goals was to be able to pass the language requirements for Canadian citizenship. At the time of their arrival, that had seemed like a distant goal. In only three years, Alia had raced across that finish line, and was still running. She amazed all of us, and even herself.

CITIZENSHIP DAY AMID A PANDEMIC

A^{l:}

A few years before the Al Rmidain family arrived in Mississauga, I retired from television broadcasting and embarked on a second career in information technology. When Carol and I joined the refugee support committee, my main role was as treasurer, but I quickly became the tech-support person, setting up a donated computer for the Al Rmidains.

Almost five years later, I was also the point person on the day of their citizenship hearing, which was conducted via video-conference.

After they completed all of their citizenship requirements, the pandemic caused significant delays in getting a date for the actual ceremony. Finally, a date was announced, with the promise that a secure link would connect them with the citizenship judge in a video conference. It would be in May, 2021.

I was happy to help get them connected for a process that had been adapted due to COVID. There was no point in trying to explain what they should expect, because none of us had any experience with on-line citizenship hearings!

Every week, across the country, dozens of immigrants are welcomed to Canadian citizenship in group ceremonies. This follows three years of residence in Canada, studying for a test on knowledge of Canada, achieving suitable language skills, interviewing and a lot of waiting for The Big Day to arrive.

Before COVID, citizenship ceremonies were held in large event centres. During the pandemic, the Canadian government developed an on-line version of the ceremony. We – that is, the Al Rmidain family's friends -- expected there would be other participating families, all tuned into the same on-line ceremony, and each waiting for the citizenship judge to speak to them in private. What we had not expected was that we were not welcome to view and participate in the on-line event. Each participating family would join the citizenship ceremony using a link which they were not supposed to share.

This news came as a disappointment to several members of the support committee, who had set aside the afternoon hoping to watch the happy ceremony. We knew that the pandemic would mean we couldn't be in the same room as the Al Rmidains, but many had expected to watch and listen on their computers, laptops or phones, and share in Alia's and Hussein's joy. We needed a solution that would not violate the rules set by the citizenship judge and staff.

On Hussein and Alia's big day, May 28, 2021, at 1:15 pm exactly, I was at their home. My job, as chief "techie" for the day, was to make sure nothing went wrong in their video connection with the citizenship judge.

The family was arrayed in their best clothes, crammed together on their sofa, facing a laptop screen. Even Musa sat for some of the time.

I found a way to allow Alia's and Hussein's friends to watch, without breaking any COVID rules or any of the conditions imposed by the Citizenship Office. From a second laptop in the room, I opened another video-conference link for Alia's and Hussein's friends to listen and watch from afar. The second laptop was aimed at the family on the sofa. It picked up the judge's remarks, and most of the sound from the official video confer-ence. Not perfect, but better than just listening in by phone. It was a sort of fly-on-the-wall level of participation.

From our vantage point, huddled in their kitchen, I along with two other friends of the family overheard the explanations of the process, the music interludes, and the long waits between steps in the process. Finally, we could hear the citizenship judge's staff preparing the Al Rmidains for their family chat with the judge.

The judge's clerk asked each one to hold their permanent resident card close to the laptop's camera. These cards had been Alia's, Hussein's and the children's primary photo identification since they arrived in Canada. Once the clerk had confirmed their names and faces, the family was intro-duced to the citizenship judge. Then the judge asked all of them, even the children, a few questions about themselves.

When those preliminaries were complete, the adults and older children were asked to recite the oath of citizenship. Next, somewhat bizarrely, the judge's staff members directed each member of the family, in view of the camera, to use scissors to cut their permanent resident cards into pieces, while the clerk watched to see that the cards were fully destroyed.

The clerk then assured the family that their new cards -- citizenship cards -- would be sent to them.

The part of the ceremony which required the Al Rmidains to be in conver-sation with the citizenship clerk and judge was fairly short. There was a lot of time for the children to roam around the house, while the judge left the conference to have a private chat with each of the other family groups. If the event had taken place pre-COVID, in a formal auditorium, it is hard to imagine Musa remaining in his chair for the whole hour and a half or more. Even for the older children and adults, the atmosphere in the Al Rmidain living room swung between eager anticipation and complete boredom.

Nonetheless the Citizenship office staff have worked hard, within COVID restraints, to retain some sense of ceremony and importance. I salute them for that!

At the conclusion, the judge left the conference, while one of the citizenship department staff congratulated the family and advised them further about the delivery of their citizenship cards. The clerk managed to convey a sincere sense of warmth. She said she and her colleagues hoped that this on-line event was both solemnly significant and joyfully celebratory.

Alia's and Hussein's friends were watching, or phoning in for progress reports, throughout the ceremony. A few of us were also quietly huddled in the Al Rmidain's kitchen, reporting to the others. We were all as excited as Alia and Hussein's family – indeed, we *were* Alia and Hussein's family, in the absence of any relatives from their homeland.

Receiving congratulations afterwards by means of emails and phone calls could not substitute for holding a citizenship celebration in a park or at a restaurant, as we would have done before COVID. So, Alia, Hussein, Ruth, Jeanine and a few others made plans to hold a citizenship party at a later date, when COVID gathering rules would be more flexible. That event happened on Saturday, September 18, 2021 on the lawn outside Clarkson Road Presbyterian Church. It was also a celebration of the Al Rmidain's fifth anniversary in Canada.

The sun shone and the breeze was light. Coronavirus restrictions on gatherings had lifted enough to permit food to be shared out-of-doors. A rainy day would have created a conflict with the COVID directives for that time in Ontario. It was a huge relief for all when the weather held.

As part of the welcome for guests at the picnic, everyone had to sign in at the COVID contact-tracing table. This marked the first time most of the guests had attended a picnic at which a contact-tracing list was required!

A long table laden with trays of food displayed the work of Alia and her friends, both her newcomer and Canadian friends. It included platters of Syrian barbeque kabobs cooked to perfection by Hussein and some Arab friends who had brought their own barbeques to the event. Beside the trays there are enormous bowls of salads and other dishes, some Arab and some Canadian. And pita bread. There can be no meal without pita, as Alia has said.

Adults and children lined up for the meal, maintaining more distance than at most outdoor, church picnics in normal times, but engaging in conversations.

Many of the volunteers and their families in attendance had not been able to visit with the Al Rmidain family since the first COVID restrictions were put in place to control the pandemic's spread in March 2020. They had not seen each other in church or at face-to-face meetings for over eighteen months. The availability of vaccines was making everyone a bit more relaxed, and able to enjoy a large gathering. Just one year earlier, having no vaccines and more uncertainty about transmission, no celebratory picnic would have been possible. It was a very happy day.

CHANGES

Ruth:

Jeanine and I were co-chairs of the team of volunteers. We began this adventure long before Alia and Hussein arrived in Canada in 2016. Both Jeanine and I consider them friends, and look forward to continuing the journey with them.

Their story is not typical of all newcomers to Canada. For one thing, Hussein's success at becoming fluent in English in just one year can be attributed to his hard work. The co-ordinator of his English language program told me that he was the best student in his year, achieving more than any other student in a relatively short period.

Secondly, his skills in both welding and vehicle repair enabled him to find work quickly. Then, in only a few months, his employer at the truck-repair shop made him his "number two" man. This meant that Hussein supervised the others, whenever the boss was away. With the increased responsibilities came longer hours, as well as more income. This has been beneficial to the family, although he is seldom at home. He now has a chance to become a licensed mechanic, which will require even more study.

Following their parents' example, the children have all been successful in school. The oldest bears the load of having two working parents, and younger siblings in need of some care and supervision after school. All the children show commitment to doing the best that they can.

The many opportunities provided to the children (choir, band, scouts, Pedalheads, skating, swimming and much more) have given them confidence to participate fully in school and community life. Their teachers have commented to me and to other volunteers that the children have richly benefitted from all of these experiences.

Finally, Alia is a remarkably strong and resilient person. She was always determined to seek the best for her children. More than that, she has set goals and challenges for herself, overcoming her natural shyness to become the person, the Canadian, she is now.

Trying to do everything, and satisfy everyone had a cost, for Alia. Syrian custom requires her to produce food at whatever hour her husband comes home, and also to feed anyone who comes to seek his advice or just to visit him in the evening. All of this is inconsistent with her retail store hours, including frequent evening shifts.

It wasn't easy for her to acknowledge that she couldn't do it all. With encouragement from me and others, she discussed this with her children, and shifted some of the housekeeping and meal preparation burden to them. Hussein has also tempered his expectations just a little.

In their own Syrian-Canadian circle, and especially among recently-arrived Syrians, Alia and Hussein are regarded as leaders. They have the obvious signs of success, having two jobs and two cars, even though their total income is very modest by Canadian standards. They can access services in English. They know people to ask, if they need to solve a problem for someone else. On sunny weekends in the summer, when groups of Syrian families meet at a lakeside park in Mississauga, others will approach them for advice and counsel.

The next years will bring challenges. They are waiting on news of Hussein's younger brother, now living in Lebanon. He has been approved for immigration to Canada, but the pandemic has caused a lengthy backlog in processing. They are very eager for him to get to Canada, and to follow Hussein's path to self-sufficiency.

I admire Alia greatly. She is timid and brave at the same time. Since I first met her, she has gained a great deal of confidence in her own abilities, bolstered by her success at learning to communicate in English. She has fears, but a strong will to face those fears. She has instilled these qualities in her children.

Amal and Ahmed are now high-school students. Amal dreams of becoming a lawyer. Her younger sister has also begun to think about university, and the possibility of law school. Ahmed is a little quieter about his goals. As yet, the family has little concept of how expensive post-secondary education can be.

Recently, Alia was promoted to assistant manager, and moved to another nearby Dollarama store. She believes the district manager may be considering her as a store manager, when she gains more experience. She is taking community college courses to improve her language skills. I could not be prouder if she were my own daughter.

As their journey in Canada continues, they will not be alone. They have friends.

POST SCRIPT

At the time of publication, Alia and Hussein had learned that Hussein'syounger brother had finally received an invitation to the Canadian embassy in Beirut to be processed for his travel to Canada. There was no information about his arrival date, but the family's excitement was building. A room in their townhouse has been set aside for Mahmoud. The Al Rmidains are eager to welcome Mahmoud, and introduce him to their Canadian family.

ACKNOWLEDGEMENTS

There were many more volunteers involved in this story than those named. Some contributed anecdotes, photographs or information but did not get their own chapter. I took the step of condensing many stories.

I recruited several friends as readers, each with different skills and experience, and I thank them for their time and contributions: First mention goes to Penny MacKenzie who suggested I toss the first draft and begin again. I did. It isn't wise to ignore the advice of retired English teachers.

Special mention goes to Ann Schweighofer for providing the idea for the book, and then proof-reading and making suggestions; to Professor Hilary Evans Cameron for amendments and enthusiasm, and to my husband, Jim Cairney, for many edits and suggestions. I must also thank Alia for agreeing to share her life in this very public way, and for sitting patiently for many hours of interviews. She and Hussein replied to my queries and text messages on a variety of questions as the book took shape.

Several of the volunteers took a great deal of time and care to proof-read my several drafts. They sent me many important corrections and suggestions. I am most grateful to them for helping Alia and me to tell her story. Some of these volunteers have been my personal friends for many years before the sponsorship began, but others are new friends for me, as they are for Alia and Hussein and the children.

The first-names-only approach was used to describe the volunteers in the narrative. This was done to preserve the anonymity of some, but makes it awkward to thank those who gave their time to be interviewed, and who later reviewed what I was going to say about them. Even so, I want them to see their names here, and I want readers to know that these are real people with huge hearts. Thank you, all of you, for your time and patience with the process of creating this book: Jeanine, Raj, Molly, Lorna, Heather, Al, Carol, Nancy, Ken, Sue, and especially Ruth. Alia still reads English slowly, to her great frustration, so Ruth met with her regularly and read aloud much of the first half of the book with Alia. Thus, over several weeks, Alia and Ruth helped me to make the story as accurate as possible.

In addition to those on the refugee support committee, many members of the two leading churches, Clarkson Road Presbyterian Church and Christ Church (since re-named Christ First) United Church, and the staff members of both churches played active roles in supporting the Al Rmidains. This includes the pastors, music directors and choir leaders, secretaries, cub and scout leaders, camp counsellors (Band Camp, Tempus4Us choir) and others. Fund-raising also happened at Sheridan United Church, while the quilts for the children's beds were created and donated by Clearview Church in Mississauga. It takes a village!

Polycultural Services of Mississauga, and the ESL (English Second Language) school, deserve special mention because they assist families like the Al Rmidains every week, month after month. Once a family or a group of families graduates or moves on, another world conflict causes new faces to line up at Polycultural's service counter. The staff there are a lifeline, and I hope they know it.

The volunteers and the Al Rmidains are grateful to the staff at the United Church of Canada's national office for administering the umbrella agreement with Immigration, Refugees and Citizenship Canada, the IRCC.

The volunteers and the family are still relying on UCC staff, and their connections with IRCC, to secure the safe arrival of Hussein's brother.

In this story, two Christian congregations stand in for all the faith communities and other groups across Canada who sponsored refugees, not only those from Syria but from other flash-points in the world, as well. To take a bow and accept thanks from the Al Rmidains and their support team, I approached two friends, Marion Pardy and Karen Horst. Each of these ministers has served in leadership of their respective national churches, and has a passion for the needs of refugees. Both of them accepted with grace and were generous with their comments. Thank you, Marion and Karen, for your support of this book.

To get this book across the finish line, (because it does become a marathon, after all) I engaged the help of Akosua Brown of What's Your Story Author Services. Akosua and her team filled the gap left by the death of my late friend and publishing coach, Steve Parton. You would not be reading this book without Akosua's work.

Thanks, also, to the volunteers who shared their photographs with me, for the book. Many more photographs might have appeared in the book, especially of the children, but for the concern that children cannot and should not waive their own privacy rights. There could also have been many more stories, so that readers could appreciate their individual personalities and qualities, their excellent manners and polite inquisitiveness, their goals and aspirations. Their stories are still unfolding, and will wait for another book.